HAUNTED FLAGSTAFF

SUSAN JOHNSON

AFTERWORD BY DR. KAREN J. RENNER

Haunted America

Published by Haunted America
A Division of The History Press
Charleston, SC
www.historypress.com

Back cover, bottom: courtesy of Freaky Foot Tours, tintype photography by Eric Retterbush.

First published 2022

Manufactured in the United States

ISBN 9781467150699

Library of Congress Control Number: 2022933324

As always, for Paul, who encouraged my weird endeavors and creative writing.

And for the team at Freaky Foot Tours—you all are the best!

CONTENTS

PREFACE

I really can't remember when I first became interested in ghosts and the afterlife. As children of the '60s, my friends and I loved Halloween and everything that went with it—dressing up, scary stories and the possibility that a witch or a monster might jump out of the shrubs and give us a fright. Until sometime in my mid-twenties, that is where I kept any curiosity I had about the darker side of life—safely locked into the last two weeks of October. When November arrived, it returned to the closet along with the fright wigs and costumes.

Fast-forward to today. While I still love Halloween and all that the season implies, I'd never lump spirits and hauntings and ghostly apparitions together with October 31. I've come to believe that the other world exists *all* the time—day and night, October through September. However, outside of organized religion and a few anthropology/psychology studies, I've found little to read on what exactly that world consists of. There's no consensus on what constitutes a spirit as opposed to a ghost and why either might be involved in a haunting. This is maddening for someone who has grown to appreciate the mysteries of our world, the eerie synchronicities and energies that make themselves known. It means that a person must create their own structure of what is true through research, listening to others' accounts and personal experience.

If this is beginning to sound too academic for a book on ghosts, don't worry. I asked a real scholar to write the afterword, while I just relate the stories. However, as a nurse with three decades of experience—a fourth of it in hospice—I have pondered the afterlife with my colleagues. Most of us have experienced some very odd if not downright eerie coincidences, usually at the time of a person's passing. When these moments occur, I find my belief in life after death is reinforced. In the context of a recent death, it seems that the person still has the energy to communicate in a kind of cryptic shorthand—an "I'm OK" or "thank you." I've come to think of this as the energy of a spirit. As for a ghost, in my mind that is another entity entirely.

I once told a podcaster that I'd never had an experience with an actual ghost but later realized I'd forgotten an incident from my thirties. I was renting a lovely little casita just outside of Phoenix, Arizona. It sat in a cluster with several adobe homes, situated at the base of Camelback Mountain. I was told by a friend that the little ranchette had been a tuberculin clinic in the early twentieth century, a place of rest and recuperation for those who suffered from the disease. One evening after work, a deep fatigue seemed to roll in on me out of nowhere. I lay across the bed, still dressed in my day clothes, and fell deeply asleep. I have no recollection of what caused me to awaken; I do remember that either I or the bed was pulsating so hard that I literally vibrated off it and onto the floor. I sat there stunned. For just a few seconds, I felt another presence permeating the room. Then I gathered my wits and ran out the door to the casita behind mine. I felt a strong need to be among the living!

While I haven't experienced anything as jarring since, I now recognize that blanket of lethargy that rolls in like a fog on those rare occasions something supernatural makes an appearance. In my life, this has occurred when a close friend or family member passed or—rarely—one of the patients I'd cared for. And while these experiences are precious, they do nothing to answer the questions I have about hauntings and ghosts. A friend or loved one's spirit saying goodbye is like that of a lingering entity in only one way—neither exists on our earthly plane.

Years ago, I began reading books by Hans Holzer and other parapsychologists to learn how they differentiated and categorized the supernatural energies in our world. I've also read articles and attended lectures by those who claim to have had near-death experiences, such as Dannion Brinkley. I've formed my own opinions about the afterlife from both experiences and information gathered. I imagine this is true for anyone who reads about the paranormal—your beliefs are important to you, even as you explore. The last chapter of *Haunted Flagstaff* looks at common myths with a bent toward debunking the more egregious ones; it's not meant to step on anyone's truths.

On a lighter note, during the early 2000s, my husband and I would look for ghost tours on our trips out of state. We went on several and found that the best ones weave the history of the town and its inhabitants in with local reports of strange lights and floating apparitions. A surprising outcome from this otherworldly hobby was that my interest in history was reignited. I'm fortunate that the place I've called home for the past thirty-odd years is steeped in colorful legends from its past since the mid-1800s. The town has preserved many of the buildings and homes that were integral to its start and that give birth to stories of present-day hauntings. This book is just a peek into Flagstaff's history, starting with the railroad in the late 1880s and looking at how the people of the 1900s lived. These stories and personalities are intertwined with the ever-present if unseen spirits that grace the town today.

As I repeat several times in the pages of *Haunted Flagstaff*, this is the Anglicized version of the town's beginnings; the Native people have walked this land for centuries. Their stories are wondrous and colorful and beyond the scope of this text. However, if you like a little recent history to whet your appetite for ghostly tales, I hope this book will satisfy your craving.

ACKNOWLEDGEMENTS

There are many people to thank—first and foremost are those who came before and who took the time to record history in the making. While they are acknowledged in the text and cited in the endnotes, so much would have been lost if Platt Cline, Richard Magnum, the Babbitts, the Riordans and others hadn't taken the time to write their observations. Alongside the people who formed the town was the paper, the *Coconino Sun*. In a book about ghosts, the spirits of these entities are enmeshed with the present; they are the echoes we hear as we walk downtown Flagstaff.

Haunted Flagstaff was the brainchild of Karen Renner. She approached me in 2019 and asked if I'd give her a tour of the local haunts downtown. As we walked and talked the route (the same that's laid out in this book), she asked if I'd like to collaborate with her. Would I! However, Dr. Renner's professional life is much more demanding than mine, and her availability was limited. And then came Covid-19, which threw a wrench in all our lives. Suffice it to say I would not have thought of either *Haunted Flagstaff* or my previous book on the Walkup family without her nudging. Karen wrote the afterword for this book, and you can read her thoughtful analysis of common myths there. Thank you, Karen.

Freaky Foot Tours' guides—past and present—are an awesome, eclectic group who have been generous in sharing the stories collected as they've led their tours through the darkened streets. Some have had a paranormal encounter (or two!) and pointed me to areas that needed further investigation. Thank you to Clare, Jed, Gracie, Leslie, Michelle, Revel, Sam, Sean and—most Dreadful of all—Dre. As said in the dedication, they are the best.

In writing this book, I've found that, while many people are eager to share stories of paranormal encounters, not everyone wants their name in print. I'm grateful to all those who told me their experiences and allowed me to record them for accuracy. Whether anonymous or cited, I treasure these peeks into the other dimension that they have encountered. Many of the stories within are from locals—shop owners, hotel managers, baristas and bartenders. A few encounters were told to me by visitors who had heard through the grapevine I was writing this book. I have not discounted anyone's story, but I do verify what details I can. So, thank you Nancy, Drew, Lisa, Joshua, Mindy, Bree, Mary, Susan, Jan, Paul, Sabine, Micky—and all the others who wanted to remain anonymous. The stories are awesome, and I hope I did them justice.

I also want to thank Megan for sharing her story of the old Walkup house. I wrote my first book about the place she called home while growing up. If I'd known then what I know now, I might not have gotten it finished. I admire her courage for sharing some very disturbing phenomena. Thank you, Megan—I've learned so much through hearing the stories of your childhood.

Haunted Flagstaff relied on numerous books, papers and articles for historical accuracy. Very early in the process, Flagstaff Public Library and the wonderful librarians within its walls helped by finding obscure sources of local lore. Thank you, Pam, Suzannah, Alexis and all the others who work there, for your help and encouragement.

Flagstaff's Write-Time Writers—of which I'm a proud member—continues to meet weekly and share our love of writing with one another. Although we had to Zoom in 2021, the contact and support kept me on track with this book. Flagstaff has a great artistic community, and our little group is part of it.

The History Press turns out beautiful books, and I'm grateful they agreed to take this one on. Thank you, Laurie Krill, and all the others who work to transform text into a lovely product.

There were many in town who went beyond just retelling a ghost story for the book. Drew Purcell took time from his busy morning at the Weatherford and gave me the top-to-bottom tour. Thank you, Drew. The same to John Propster and Suzanne Casale, who literally took me behind the scenes at Theatrikos. Molly Baker, marketing director for the Orpheum, made room in her busy schedule and allowed me access to the balcony and stage areas. She also shared a story or two—thank you, Molly! Joshua Hudlow's card states he's a visitor services specialist, and he lives up to the title. He's obviously a ghost hunter at heart, but in his day job at the Visitors Center, he led me through the maze of doors and stairways and had a story for every area in the building. Thank you, Josh. And thank you to Lisa, another Visitors Center staff member, for your gentle story of Hopi quiet time and spirits from the past.

The last of the thank-yous go to my family and friends. My son Nick may or may not believe in ghosts, but he kept my spirits up during the lonely process of actually writing this book. And my long-distance friends and Zoom buddies managed a polite inquiry into its progress, even though some didn't quite know what to think about the subject!

Before ending the acknowledgements and moving on to the stories, I have to say that the town has many more historic sites that deserve to be investigated. I've heard rumors that the old courthouse has a ghost or two, as well as the nearby DPS building. Flagstaff's Downtown Diner is another place often mentioned as haunted. South of the tracks, buildings that were once brothels have been transformed into business suites, but renters say the former clientele still hang around. Citizens Cemetery, across from NAU, is beautifully maintained and the many historic graves deserve a book unto themselves. The cemetery is open to the public but closes at sunset, and while it's peaceful during the daylight, it can become quite eerie as dusk approaches. There are other places as well...but they'll have to wait for another book.

Introduction

This is the Anglicized story of Flagstaff, the little settlement in the mountains of Northern Arizona that survived to become a town with ghosts rather than a ghost town. The land is rich with the history of Native American peoples—the Navajo and Hopi tribes, the Anasazi, the Sinagua and many more. It's not within the scope of *Haunted Flagstaff* to tell their stories beyond some instances where the cultures intersect. There are fascinating and well-researched tomes available for those wanting to dig into the history of the Native population, and I urge you to search them out.

For the purposes of this book, the reader will be introduced to the Flagstaff of the late 1800s through the mid-1900s. The town fathers (yes, they were mostly business*men* in those days) recognized the area's potential and possessed the skills that would guide it to growth and prosperity. Their names are still in evidence today: the Babbitts, Tim and Michael Riordan, Thomas McMillian, John Weatherford—the list is a long one. They invested in the community by building churches, schools and infrastructure. And while there were few women at the helm of local businesses back then, many played prominent roles within the town's overall fabric.

Much of Flagstaff's stability came first from the environment—the large ponderosa pine forest that supported the lumber mills, the cool mountain air that beckoned visitors throughout the summer and the geological wonders that drew scientists from around the world. This is not hyperbole. Many of the railroad settlements that sprang up as the gandy dancers laid a westward track seemingly disappeared overnight as the camps moved on. Flagstaff managed to dig in and carve out an economic path for the town that allowed it to build on itself. One of the first industries, processing lumber for railroad ties, buildings and so on, gave birth to a stable population that allowed for the Teacher's College, Lowell Observatory and tourism to take root.[1]

Walking through downtown in 2022, you can still sense the Flagstaff of the 1900s. Many of the landmarks are the same, although some have been repurposed. Dr. Raymond's former home and office comes to mind; it's been both a photography and yoga studio, as well as a general store. The old courthouse remains standing; it was built in 1894 and served the town until 2020. Other buildings, like the Hotel Monte Vista and the Weatherford, have remained open year-round for overnight guests. These structures—modernized and renovated over the decades—are where the history of the town and stories of ghosts intersect. Many of the buildings are easily identified in the decades-old black-and-white photographs that decorate their walls today.

If you live here or have visited lately, you'll notice the chapters are laid out as if one is taking a stroll downtown on Aspen Street. Arguably, this is the heart of Flagstaff, where parades were (and are) held and shops sprang up as the population increased. Aspen itself is also easy to place in images from the early 1900s. Several of the haunts are located a few blocks north or south of the main route, but for the most part, the stories within *Haunted Flagstaff* are centered downtown. The exception is chapter 10, which identifies several paranormal hotspots suggested by ghost-hunting enthusiasts that are scattered throughout the city.

So, cozy up in an armchair with your favorite beverage and travel back in history on a paranormal adventure. You'll meet some of the men and women who once walked the town and imbued it with their character. Those of us who roam the streets today can sense their spirits, if not always see them. Come take a stroll through Flagstaff—the good, the bad and the eerie.

CHAPTER 1
A SMALL MOUNTAIN TOWN

In the mid-1800s, President James Polk saw the appropriation of Texas as necessary for the United States' westward expansion. This resulted in the Mexican-American War, which ended in 1848. In 1850, the Territory of New Mexico was formed and included the land that is now both New Mexico and Arizona. Interestingly, the Arizona Territory was formed by a vertical split of the landmass in 1863 by the congressional Arizona Organic Act, which also abolished slavery in the new region. Arizona later became the forty-eighth state admitted to the Union, on Valentine's Day 1912. This feat was not accomplished without some bickering and ugly innuendos being tossed at the new state's supporters. It's been said that Theodore Roosevelt was wary of the sparsely populated and dry lands in the Southwest; he was also not too keen on the cantankerous individuals who lived here. However, after much diplomacy and bargaining, the boundaries were drawn and the deed was done.[2]

The differences between the northern region and southern region of the state are startling to those who haven't visited. Generally speaking, from New River south to its border with Mexico, Arizona is a flat, dry desert, its rugged terrain dotted with cacti and sagebrush. Summers are extremely hot and long, with three to four months of mild temperatures during the winter. From Cordes Junction northward, the state couldn't be more different. While desert plants are still visible, they begin to mingle with pine and spruce on the climb up to the Colorado Plateau. The air remains dry in the high country, but there are four to five seasons to the year, and skiing at Humphreys Peak or in the White Mountains is a winter pastime.

Humphreys Peak, located in the Kachina Peaks Wilderness, towers over the city of Flagstaff and has become iconic in the town's image. *Author's collection.*

The cultural differences that were present in the mid-1800s were even more pronounced. Travel within the territory was dangerous and difficult, and the populations didn't commingle as freely as in some states. Southern Arizona was still the Wild West, with boomtowns encroaching on Apache and Mexican lands and frequent skirmishes settled by gunfights. In the 1860s, the area that is now part of Tucson endured several years as the Confederate Arizona Territory. Northern Arizona, while still claiming its share of gunslingers, had by the 1880s developed into a more diverse landscape. The region was an oasis for those who valued mountains, greenery, fresh air and space. By most accounts, the sheepherders and farmers who first settled the northlands welcomed the railroad and the lumber mills and the workers who followed. One gets the impression that the northern part of the territory—through necessity and having common goals—found cooperation with others a laudable virtue.

While many small western towns went bust, Flagstaff grew and flourished. Central to its longevity is the town's geography. Situated inside the largest contingent ponderosa pine forest west of the Mississippi, Flagstaff had a seemingly endless supply of lumber in the years that entire towns were made from wood. It was also surrounded by historic ruins and geological wonders that earned it the title "The City of Seven Wonders." With the Grand Canyon ninety miles to the north and Oak Creek Canyon thirty miles south, tourism became a vital industry right alongside ranching and processing lumber.

Along with these natural blessings, Flagstaff can trace its growth to several fortuitous events. The arrival of the railroad was a game-changer for the whole of the United States, especially those who lived in the West. The changes that occurred were rapid and radically affected those living in Northern Arizona. The wet, snowy winters and cold mountain air—part of the climate that made the area desirable—also isolated its inhabitants and made it difficult to drive livestock to market. However, once the Atlantic-Pacific began to run at least somewhat reliably through the area, commerce improved, money was made and adventurous folk became enamored of the lands out West. The community of Flagstaff, while admittedly isolated by geography, was not isolationist at heart. Residents mostly welcomed the changes being made, as reported in the pages of the *Coconino Sun*, and the town became even more progressive and established.[3]

Looking north up San Francisco in 1943 from the railroad. Babbitt's store is up the street on the left, and the Hotel Monte Vista is on the right. *Library of Congress online catalogue, photographer Jack Delano.*

Speaking of the *Sun*, the weekly newspaper was a fount of knowledge on all things within and without the small town. Scrolling through issues from the early 1900s, the reader meets the citizenry, including the outlaws and the lawmen. One can follow the building of the Weatherford Hotel and Majestic Opera House, as well as the comings and goings of Dr. Raymond and the Babbitts. From the start, education was on the minds of the town founders, and when Emerson School was opened in 1895, there was a parade down Aspen accompanied by speeches and refreshments. As the town grew in size and importance, people wanted a modern hotel to compete with the Harvey Houses. That was the impetus for today's Monte Vista hotel, or the Monte V as it's affectionately known. Suffice it to say that many of today's local haunts had their beginnings in the early 1900s, and one can trace that history in the pages of the *Coconino Sun*.[4]

Twenty-first-century Flagstaff is still a bustling city, with a population close to seventy-five thousand and a state university that adds another twenty thousand. Tourism remains an important industry, although Northern Arizona University (NAU) and several large businesses (W.L. Gore, for one) are also major employers. Old-timers are aware of the urban sprawl that has steadily encroached on the mesas and into the forests; however, the town still has the vague feel of isolation that it possessed one hundred years ago. Perhaps it's this loneliness that defines the area and gives rise to so many of the haunted stories that follow.

CHAPTER 2

FLAGSTAFF PUBLIC LIBRARY, THE SITE OF THE OLD EMERSON SCHOOL

Slightly west of city hall and across Aspen Street is the main branch of the Flagstaff Public Library. The building itself was erected in 1986 on the grounds of the old Emerson School, which had closed several years earlier. Locals who patronize it and librarians who work within its walls tell stories of disembodied heads that float among the stacks and a children's room prone to overnight mischief. Whether these occurrences stem from the site's previous history as the school or its present incarnation is up for debate.

To appreciate the importance of Emerson School, one must understand the town's earliest conception of itself. Two of Flagstaff's leading families, the Babbitts and the Riordans, were well educated, and they intended to steer the town in a lofty direction. As early as the 1890s, they and other involved citizens cast the community as one that welcomed scientists, teachers and regular, hardworking folk. The leaders knew that stability and safety would attract the kind of people who shared their values. To be sure, there were still those characters who preferred a rough-and-tumble lifestyle. However, they were becoming a minority as steady work prevailed and families grew. The town fathers set about creating the environment they envisioned, and after building a jail and a courthouse, the issue of a proper school was addressed in an 1894 town meeting.

According to local historian Platt Cline, Emerson High School was named in honor of poet Ralph Waldo Emerson. The two-story building, made with red brick and native red sandstone, opened to 155 students on September 19, 1895. The structure cut an imposing figure, and at its first

The sidewalk leading to the main doors of the Flagstaff Public Library, downtown branch. The entrance is directionally close to where Emerson School's front doors were. *Author's collection.*

commencement in April 1897, the crowds overflowed into the hallways. When the Normal School (now NAU) opened its doors in 1899, Emerson defaulted to becoming an elementary school. By 1912, the school was so crowded that four more classrooms were added, as well as hardwood floors and indoor drinking fountains.[5]

As with the rickety wooden building that preceded it, Emerson was used for more than just teaching children their studies. The school became a community center where people gathered for after-hours educational programs, meetings and the occasional party. As the population grew and diversified, other schools followed. However, the Emerson School maintained its position in town for almost nine decades, serving the students of Flagstaff from 1895 until 1985.

In 1986, the distinguished if deserted red brick building was demolished to make way for the lot's present occupant, the Flagstaff Public Library. While the library is sleek and modern, looking nothing like Emerson, the new building does share part of the latter's foundation. Former students, now in their sixties and seventies, have said the basement at the old school gave them the creeps.

"It was naturally dark and full of tables, desks and chairs stacked on top of each other," said one former student, who asked not to be identified. "The whole building was pretty eerie, especially after hours. I never liked staying late for club meetings, especially in the winter."

This man denied ever seeing a ghost or apparition during his school days but felt the way the building was laid out might have given rise to stories of paranormal experiences. "It was an old building, with large rooms. Footsteps literally echoed in the hallways, and your voice would bounce off the walls."

There is a legend of a haunting that has circulated for the past three decades and grew out of the musty depths of the shared basement. I've done the research and found no evidence to back up any actual historical event that the story is based on. I'll recount it below, however, because of its persistence and its presence in the city's own ghost-walk literature. This is the story of Emerson the ghost:[6]

> *One winter in the early 1900s, the principal of Emerson School arrived at the building to find the front door locked. This was unusual, as it was the job of the janitor to get to school a half hour early, unlock the door and, in the wintertime, go down to the basement and fire up the furnace. Until this day, the janitor had been conscientious and reliable in his duties. The principal, having his own set of keys, was able to let himself inside the frigid building. Not finding the janitor on any floor, the man went downstairs to start the furnace. It's said that even then the basement was a dark, overcrowded storage room that was difficult to maneuver through. However, the principal began to make his way through the stacked desks and toward the large heater in the far corner. Coming to a blind aisle, he turned and was hit in his upper body by something hanging from one of the large pipes running the length of the ceiling. Grabbing at the offending item, the principal recoiled in horror when he realized he had hold of a man's leg. It took a few long moments for the startled man to gather his wits and take a closer look. When he did, he saw that the leg dangling in the air did indeed belong to the absentee janitor.*

The story continues with the sheriff arriving and then trudging through the snow to the deceased man's address. It was his sad duty to inform the janitor's wife that she was now his widow:

> *When he arrived at the small white home, it was evident that something was amiss. It was much too quiet for a household that should be up, preparing for the day. When no one answered the sheriff's persistent knocking, he went around the house, peering through the windows. It was through one at the*

> *back that he caught a glimpse of the dead man's wife, fully dressed and laid out on the bed. She appeared to have been strangled and was obviously dead. Moving to another window, the sheriff saw the figures of two little girls inside, both with the same ugly welts around their necks. Sadly, no notes nor indications of what drove the janitor to kill his family and then himself were discovered.*

Again, no research has been found to confirm the story of Emerson School's murderous janitor, although the tale contains whiffs of the Walkup family tragedy. Regardless, according to locals and librarians past and present, the Flagstaff Public Library may be the most haunted building in downtown. Shortly after it opened in 1986, a hazy mist that somewhat resembled a man climbing invisible stairs was seen in the northwest corner of the building. This particular apparition has been reported several times throughout the years, although not lately. Instead, recent sightings center on the reference books and the children's section.

I spoke with Mary, a young woman who held a part-time job at the library several years ago. While she has moved on in her professional life, incidents she encountered while scanning and shelving books have stayed with her. A seemingly no-nonsense businesswoman with a quirky sense of humor, she was willing to share some of her stories with me about her time at the downtown library:

> *When I was working there, about ten years ago, the library wasn't open on Sundays. So, two people would be scheduled to work a few hours doing all the "clean-up" the librarians couldn't get to during the week. We'd have to track down mis-shelved books, re-sort the magazines and papers—things like that. I always hated to work on Sundays because there was a time that some really weird things were happening inside that building.*

Before going further, I want to say that over the course of these conversations, I also spoke with one of her contemporaries, who agreed with Mary's incredible stories. To continue:

> *Often—so, not every Sunday but more than just a few—when we'd unlock the doors and go inside, there would be this oppressive air inside the building. Whenever I felt that, I just knew the children's library would be a mess. It was like someone had thrown a temper tantrum inside the room. Each time was different, but I saw piles of books scattered about, overturned Lego*

Side view of the library, taken from across Aspen. The notorious children's section lies behind the row of windows that are visible. *Author's collection.*

> *projects that someone took hours putting together, just broken into pieces on the floor.... The papier-mâché animals that hang from the ceilings—we'd find them on their heads or sides in the back of the aisles.*

When I asked Mary if it frightened her, since the destruction had been done before she arrived, she said:

> *Oh yeah! And remember, it's not just me. We worked in pairs on Sundays—probably because no one would go in there alone for half the day. But whenever the children's room was a mess, it felt like whoever or whatever had destroyed the room was still there. It's hard to explain, but it felt creepy in there. It almost felt like a pair of eyes were watching as we'd straighten the area up again—and those eyes did not want us in there!*

As eerie as that story is, what Mary said next is even more chilling:

> *The worst experience I ever had was while I was back in the reference stacks, shelving books from the cart. It was a Sunday, of course, and I remember I was daydreaming a bit while I went about my work. Anyway, I had a really big volume to put back—I remember the shelf was almost eye-level—and when I picked it up and turned to slide it in, I saw the meanest,*

> *ugliest, angriest disembodied head floating right in front of me, in the space the book was supposed to go.*

Mary said she screamed, which caused her co-worker to come running over to the stacks. Shaken, she told the other worker what she had seen, and while knowing it was in vain, they both checked the aisles in the reference area, as well as the whole library. No one else was in the locked building.

> *I know it sounds unbelievable, but I saw what I saw. No one could dream up that face! It was a man's—or at least, had been. I told a few people and more over the years, but really, people who have worked in the library—they know. Very strange, paranormal-type activity happens there, even today. Items on one desk disappear and turn up on the desk across the room, lights turn off and on for no apparent reason....I had a book appear out of nowhere, that had been checked out* twenty years earlier *and had basically been forgotten about....Really crazy stuff!*

I spoke with another librarian who had retired a few years before. I told her some of Mary's stories and she listened intently, then smiled. "I've had books disappear on me—and pencils and pens....I've never seen a floating head, but I don't doubt her. The library definitely has a haunted vibe to it."

This woman put forth an interesting theory that I hadn't heard before:

> *I've often wondered if some of the pranks are caused by a few of our former patrons. Ever since I can remember, the library has opened its doors to Flagstaff's homeless. As long as they obeyed the rules, people were welcomed to sit inside by the fire or in the air conditioning until closing. It's changed because of Covid—which is a shame. For many of the indigent, the library was the closest thing to a home they had. It would not surprise me if their spirits returned after they passed, if only because it's so familiar to them. We all were a bit like family.*

This last analysis struck a chord of truth with me. I've done exterior investigations around the library's parking lot and perimeter. We never did a session inside the building itself, but the surrounding area registers abnormally high electromagnetic activity. I accompanied another group of ghost hunters who captured several large orbs while in the library's parking lot, one of which seemed to be following a man deliberately. We tried capturing EVPs (electronic voice phenomena) that night, but none was

A view of the library across its parking lot. Ghost hunters come here to capture images of orbs, and the old hanging tree is said to have been in the north corner of the lot. *Author's collection.*

credible enough to publish. However, these oddities along with firsthand reports from staff have solidified the library in my mind as one of downtown's paranormal hotspots.[7]

One other historical tidbit might explain some of the sightings around the building. Before the railroad, when Flagstaff was little more than a handful of saloons and a general store, frontier justice was sometimes found at the end of a rope. The old hanging tree is said to have been located near the north corner of the library's parking lot. Asphalt and cement sidewalks cover the site today, but one can imagine that the spirits of the rustlers and thieves may return on occasion. Stories of blinking lights and low whistling coming from that corner persist. Many local ghost hunters believe this area is "more haunted" than a few blocks east, where the hotels and bars are located. I've seen pictures of orbs captured in the north parking lot that are compelling, especially when paired with strong EMF (electromagnetic force) readings. Whether due to its history or local legends, the land around the old Emerson School has intrigued paranormal investigators for years.[8]

CHAPTER 3
THE ORPHEUM AND THE MAJESTIC OPERA HOUSE

Several blocks east of the library on Aspen sits the Orpheum Theatre. This historic venue is used today for concerts, movies and parties of all kinds—much as it was a century ago. The building is just west of the Weatherford Hotel and bears a startling resemblance to its predecessor, the Majestic Opera House. To read the history behind these two theaters is to learn the story of one of Flagstaff's legendary—if eccentric—founders, John Weatherford.

John W. Weatherford was born in Fort Worth, Texas, in 1859 into a somewhat prominent family. When he was six, they moved twenty-five miles west to a settlement that later became Weatherford, Texas. John W. must have had an adventurous streak, as he eventually left Texas and headed farther west to Arizona. In 1887, he gained local fame as a member of the posse involved in one gruesome episode of the Pleasant Valley War. According to the Weatherford Hotel's website, the young deputy rode into town "to dispel rumors of killing among the posse that had been trying to settle the Graham-Tewkesbury feud." This long-running war between the two families was legendary, and Weatherford's participation in even one showdown bought him credibility with Arizonians.

After taking stock of the town, Weatherford quickly set down roots in Flagstaff. He was elected justice of the peace in 1887 and, three years later, clerked for the first Coconino County supervisor. He accumulated wealth by running livestock and opened a general store on the site where the Weatherford Hotel still stands. This was an ambitious young man, and we'll get into the story of his hotel in the next chapter. Suffice it to say, he was a visionary. Weatherford opened the Majestic Opera House in 1911, about eleven years after his hotel was established.[9]

There had already been an opera house in Flagstaff. In the late 1890s, the Babbitt brothers opened one bearing the family name, and it staged musical events, parties and gatherings of all sorts. It also showed the first moving picture in Flagstaff in 1897. After hosting a memorable turn-of-the-century New Year's Eve Gala in 1899, the brothers decided to convert the building into a furniture store. Movies were still shown on occasion at the Bank Hotel Hall, but it was evident the town needed another theater. Flagstaff was becoming a popular layover spot as travel increased and visitors to the Grand Canyon caught the stagecoach heading north from here. Weatherford, who had his finger on the pulse of the town's hospitality industry (such that it was in 1910), responded by building the Majestic.

Photographs of the Majestic Opera House show a boxy wooden building with plenty of windows. The streets were packed dirt in the early 1900s, and instead of cars driving past, one sees horses and wagons. The Majestic continued the tradition of the Babbitts' former venue by hosting parties, symphonies, plays and moving pictures. There was an underground tunnel connecting the Majestic to the Weatherford Hotel. John W. did not want his guests to suffer wet feet and chilled bones as they walked from one building to the other in the wintertime.

A record-breaking snowstorm in December 1915 bought an end to the Majestic, while the town itself narrowly avoided a catastrophe. Flagstaff's grand New Year's Eve party was planned for Thursday, December 30. According to Platt Cline, a winter storm brought heavy, wet snow to the region that fell throughout the day. However, the festivities remained on for that evening with a big party at the Majestic, a favorite of the locals. The revelers said goodnight well after midnight and trudged home through the drifts. Sometime around 6:00 a.m., people awoke to the loud cracking and clattering of falling timber. Those that could shoveled a path into town and gathered in front of what remained of the Majestic. Its roof and sides had caved in from the weight of some sixty inches of snow, leaving it flattened like a pancake. It didn't escape notice that, had the building fallen five hours earlier, many of Flagstaff's good citizens would have been buried in its rubble. While the town bemoaned the loss of the popular venue, John Weatherford vowed to rebuild it. He managed to salvage the movie projector, and moving pictures continued to be shown, courtesy of Babbitt's garage, until the new theater was raised.

Left: The downstairs bathroom inside the Orpheum has long been rumored to be the site of strange phenomena, including faucets that turn on and off at will. *Author's collection.*

Below: An outside view of the Orpheum, with the Weatherford's cupola (or witch's cap) looming in the background. *Courtesy Freaky Foot Tours, tintype photography by Eric Retterbush.*

Weatherford kept his promise, and in August 1917, the Orpheum Theatre opened where the Majestic once stood. While the building has been remodeled and upgraded many times, photographs from the early 1900s depict the Orpheum looking much like it does today. The venue resumed showing motion pictures and hosting music, dances and civic events. As noted on the Weatherford Hotel's website, the Orpheum allowed an actual elephant onto its stage, an act unrepeated by any other venue in town. Through the decades, the theater was also used to sell war bonds, educate the public and celebrate the town as it redefined itself and its position in Arizona.

The Orpheum in 2022 is making up for time lost to the pandemic of 2020–21. It has carefully reopened to seasonal events, much to the relief of the locals and college kids who have missed the theater's unique shows and laid-back atmosphere. Walking up to the box office, one is reminded of the stand-alone theaters from the '60s and '70s. An old-fashioned marquee advertises coming attractions, and colorful posters cover the outside windows. As the patron steps inside the small lobby, there is both a candy counter and popcorn stand. To the right, a short hallway leads toward two public bathrooms and a stairway that ascends to the balcony. (One of the bathrooms and the balcony are sites of paranormal experiences.) If the patron goes straight into the theater proper, she's greeted by a cavernous space that is adapted to whatever event is being held. A full bar is to one's right, and an audience can be seated at tables interspersed with chairs or in the area closer to the stage. Walking into the Orpheum after hours, it's striking how spacious the arena both is and feels. At the same time, there's an intimacy that comes with being able to see the balcony, the stage and all but the lobby when one stands near the bar downstairs.

I spoke to the manager, Susan, in the spring of 2021 about reported hauntings inside the theater:

> *I have to admit I haven't seen or really even felt anything that has frightened me inside the building. We do have trouble with the lights during some shows—and there's never a good explanation for why. The overhead lights on the trackers near the stage—sometimes they have a mind of their own. They go on and off, or they'll start flickering in the middle of a show—that kind of thing. We've had the wiring checked by electricians—none of them ever found a solid reason for it.*

Looking down on the stage from the balcony area. At the back of the balcony, near what was the projectionist's booth, there's a tunnel leading to the marquee out front. A man was said to have jumped from there and died. *Author's collection.*

A story that has long circulated regards a ghostly apparition that is sighted in the balcony, sitting among the audience during a live show. When I asked Susan if she'd had any direct experience with this spirit, she said no. However, I did speak with a local woman who had a tale to share, although she did not want her name used:

> *This happened a while ago, around 2012. I was at the Orpheum with friends to see a concert, and we had seats in the balcony. There were four or five of us, and we were at the end of a row. There was one empty space at the very end, the aisle seat, which I thought was weird. I said something to the others, and my friend said it was probably kept open for the usher to use during the show. That made sense, so I forgot about it and sat back to enjoy the music. Sometime during the performance, I looked away from the stage. My eyes were tired, so I looked around and down the row and saw a woman sitting in the aisle seat. She was about four spaces away from me,*

> *and I didn't think anything about it for a few seconds. But* something *about her must have been off because I turned and looked back again, and no one was there. It startled me at first, then freaked me out—I know I saw a woman sitting there. When the music was over, I asked my friend sitting next to the empty seat who was next to her during the song, and she looked at me like I was crazy. I've thought about that night more than once....I'm not sure why I turned and looked that second time. I think it was because the woman seemed translucent somehow.*

While stories of a ghostly woman roaming the balcony persist, this version is the only one I've been told directly. In "Flagstaff's Haunted Places," James Hardy wrote about a former janitor who saw a "dark figure" moving back and forth in the balcony area. It was nighttime, and the man was cleaning up after a show. When he went upstairs to investigate, no one was found. Hardy did write that there's a crawl space near the top of the balcony that leads outside to the marquee. It's been said that decades ago, a man died by suicide there. However, Hardy also wrote that no evidence could be found to support that incident.

Among the rows of seats in the Orpheum's balcony, the spirit of a woman is said to float about and sometimes take the end chair to sit and watch the show. *Author's collection.*

A closer look at the Orpheum's stage. You can see the overhead lights that have been known to flicker, track and otherwise operate on their own accord on occasion—without cause. *Author's collection.*

One of the bathrooms in the lobby also figures into the building's haunted lore. Once designated as a men's room and now a unisex facility, this restroom has a faucet that turns on and off spontaneously. The toilet paper has also been known to unroll and roll up again on the spool by itself. Various explanations have been discounted, such as vibrations from a passing train or from bass music inside the venue. The reports of these phenomena occurred mostly in the 1990s and early 2000s; Orpheum staff haven't heard any bathroom stories from patrons in the past several years.

In speaking with theater staff and going through the building during off hours, there's no denying a subtle, shadowy atmosphere that permeates the Orpheum. The employees I've spoken with have not seen apparitions or experienced supernatural plumbing problems in the restrooms. However, each admitted that—on occasion—they've felt an unseen presence in the room that follows them about with a sense of curiosity. In November 2021, television's *Dead Files* filmed a double episode that encompassed several businesses in downtown Flagstaff. The big reveal was staged at the

Orpheum, and I wondered if the staff noticed an increase in paranormal activity with all the attention.

"Not really," one person said. "If we do have a ghost—and I think we might have a quiet one—they took it in stride just like they do all the shows that are staged here."[10]

CHAPTER 4
THE WEATHERFORD HOTEL

Directly to the east of the Orpheum—and once connected by an underground passageway—is the Weatherford Hotel. A brief history of John Weatherford was given in chapter 3, so I will not repeat that part of his bio. However, hanging in the hotel's lobby is a large, framed black-and-white photograph of the man himself. The portrait shows a gentleman who looks to be about forty with a strong, handsome face and a mischievous glint in his eyes.

By all accounts, Weatherford was a real character around town, known for his far-reaching ideas. One of his most ambitious projects (some would say costliest) was to build a toll road up into the San Francisco Peaks. What started as a dream in 1914 faced many setbacks, from World War I to the Depression to Weatherford's near-bankruptcy over the whole scheme. Finally, in August 1926, with ten miles of the fourteen planned for completed, the road was opened to sightseers. According to Platt Cline, Weatherford continued to push construction, and in 1928, he made roughly $52,000 from tolls collected. By that year, the man was sixty-eight years old, and his health was not robust. He died six years later, poorer from his costly obsession but possibly pleased overall on a life lived fully.[11]

Besides hosting overnight guests, the Weatherford also receives national recognition for the Great Pinecone Drop, an annual event occurring on New Year's Eve. Started in 1999, the celebration has expanded to a family-friendly party that includes music, Santa Claus, food vendors and a 10:00 p.m. drop for those with young children. The very first pinecone was little more than a large garbage can decorated with a few strings of lights. Today, the cone is a piece of art with aluminum petals and LED lighting, and it is automatically lowered by a system of wires.

Locally, the Weatherford is known for having two of the town's favorite bars. One of them, the Zane Grey Ballroom, is located on the third floor of the hotel. This unique and historic venue embodies the feel of old Flagstaff. The Zane Grey is actually two rooms separated by a wall and joined by multiple entryways. The well-stocked bar was imported from Tombstone and is an antique Brunswick with stained-glass inlay. Three arched mirrors dominate the back wall, reflecting the light from the outside balcony back inside. Polished wooden floors that creak in just the right places make the room highly atmospheric. The ballroom is open and spacious, with a large fireplace and cheerful wallpaper that impart comfort along with a feeling of timelessness. Named in honor of the great writer who frequented the hotel, the Zane Grey has a history and a haunting behind it.

The Weatherford Hotel is known year-round as a spirited establishment, and for Halloween, the lobby is decorated accordingly. *Author's collection.*

Grey was possibly the most popular writer of western novels in his day. Born in Ohio in 1872, the young man was a good athlete and drawn to the unconventional. In college, he was torn between professional baseball and writing as a vocation. Perhaps due to his father's influence, Grey grudgingly settled on dentistry as a sensible occupation to support himself and his future family. However, the writer inside still lived, and when he opened a dental practice in New York City, it was with an eye toward the publishing houses there. When he met and married Lina Roth, her inheritance gave him the ability to quit dentistry and devote himself full time to his writing.[12]

Grey became a prolific writer of the western genre, and his bestselling book, *Riders of the Purple Sage*, was made into a successful movie. Comparing him to Stephen King today is probably over the top, but Grey did continue to be a prolific writer until his death in 1939. During the 1910s and '20s, Grey's name often popped up in the *Coconino Sun* while enjoying an extended stay at the Weatherford. It's said he wrote *The Call of the Canyon* while staying here with his entourage, as well as being inspired to start several other books.

This antiqued Brunswick bar, acquired from Tombstone, found a home at the Weatherford. One of the bartenders at the Zane Grey, Britt, has shared stories of the eerie phenomena and sightings occurring upstairs. *Author's collection.*

Zane Grey was a tireless promoter of Flagstaff and Northern Arizona and was often cited in the *Sun* as urging the town to secure a good water supply. Grey foresaw the impact tourism would have on the area, and some say that in his later years, he regretted his part in encouraging it.[13]

Before telling the stories involving the ballroom and bar, I want to relay a strange tale told to me by a local shop owner about a painting that hangs near the stairway. It's been there for years, and some call it the "Cowboy Painting." As you might expect, the painting shows a lone cowboy on horseback, dwarfed by the towering mesas and open range surrounding him. Anyone taking the stairway from the hotel lobby to the bar upstairs passes it as they go from one floor to the other. Following is the story I was told:

> *This happened around 2015. I had closed my shop and walked over to the Weatherford to meet a friend for a drink. I walked upstairs to the Zane Grey, but she hadn't arrived yet....Since there was no one I knew at the bar, I decided to go downstairs and wait for her. I was going down the steps when I noticed the painting of the cowboy that has hung on that wall there forever. I don't know why I was drawn to it that evening, but there was nothing sinister about it. I wanted to get a better look, and so I stood there, admiring the picture. I was casually wondering if that cowboy was really supposed to be Zane Grey on horseback. As I stood there alone on the stairs, a male voice suddenly whispered in my ear, "You must tell the story." It scared the hell out of me—I think I jumped a foot in the air! It might have been, "You must tell* my *story"—that part is hazy—but the rest was crystal clear.*

The woman went on to say she was so shocked and frightened by the experience that even though she's never acted on stage, she signed up for a slam poetry reading so she could fulfill the strange directive.[14]

With year-round activities and parties, the Weatherford is known as a place that attracts ghosts. Some of the stories have haunted the hotel for decades, while others (like the one just related) are told mostly by the locals. Probably the best-known tale, occurring sometime in the 1930s, is that of the unfortunate honeymooners who came to Flagstaff by train and stayed in room 54. The newlyweds had checked into their room and then were not seen for several days. While this might not seem *too* unusual, the staff did begin to wonder how the couple subsisted without some food and drink. When repeated knocks on the door went unanswered, the manager opened the door with a master key. The scene that greeted him was anything but

Left: This third-floor hallway leads away from the Zane Grey toward hotel rooms and the infamous linen closet, room 54. *Author's collection.*

Below: One of the most durable tales involves the bride and her groom found dead inside room 54. Today, it is a laundry room/linen closet, but employees still say music and low voices have been heard coming from within at night. *Author's collection.*

romantic. Lying on the bed, in her modest wedding dress, was the body of the young bride. She had been strangled, presumably by her groom, whose body was slumped over the arm of the chair that was next to the bed. A pistol lay on the floor beneath his lifeless right hand, and his temple bore the mark of a bullet.

Over the years, the story of the newlyweds in room 54 has been embellished. In some versions, the couple arrived at the hotel already bickering and staff reported hearing their voices through the closed door of their room. Another account has the young couple deeply in love and holding their wedding reception at the Zane Grey Ballroom. After dancing and dining with guests, the newlyweds retired to room 54 for their wedding night. When no one emerged from the room after two days, the manager used his pass key to investigate. Upon entering the suite, he found the young bride and groom laid out on the bed. Both had been killed by gunshot wounds to the head and died instantly. In this case, murder was suspected as the cause of death. Those favoring this version believe a jilted suitor was present at the wedding reception, or at least in the hotel. Later that night, disguised as an employee, he slipped into the room and killed the unfortunate couple.

Whatever the truth of room 54's past, the room has been repurposed and is currently used as a linen closet/storage area. Staff have reported complaints from overnight guests on that floor, usually involving sounds of arguments, low murmurings and music heard outside the room. Strangely, when any have ventured into the hallway to investigate, the sounds stop. This jives with the report of one former employee who had this to tell me:

> *One of our duties at night was to walk down the halls every hour, just to be sure everything was okay. The hallway on the third floor, just north of the bar…I really think there was something roaming around up there. It's hard to describe, but it felt electric—like the air was charged. Not every night, but enough that I didn't like walking it. Some nights I'd be standing where the bar is—getting ready to turn down the hall—and I'd hear music coming from that direction. It sounded like music from a transistor radio—kind of tinny. And when I walked toward it, the music stopped. A few times, I really thought it was coming from behind the door of the linen closet. I'd unlock the door and check, but there was never a radio inside—never anything but sheets and blankets.*

That employee's account is not the only one describing eerie noises and strange happenings at the Weatherford. A young woman who was employed there in 2015 shared a frightening story. Her mother was visiting from Phoenix, and the woman was able to comp her a room at the hotel. The two had a pleasant evening and then made plans to meet for breakfast in the morning. The following day, they sat down, and after ordering, her mother leaned across the table and said, "You know, honey, the hotel you're working in is haunted."

The younger woman told me she was so surprised she almost spilled her coffee. "I never told my mother anything about the legends associated with the Weatherford. And, really, I never thought any of that was true; I've never heard or felt anything supernatural, even when I worked nights." She went on with her story:

> *I asked my mom why she said that. She told me that she woke up around 2:00 a.m. with the feeling something was off. She looked down at the foot of her bed and saw a figure of a woman sitting there—and she looked like she was crying. She didn't hear anything, but she could tell the figure was distressed. Mom said the spirit was very airy and white, like a smoky form that didn't have features but still looked like a female. When I asked my mom if she was scared, she said no but that she felt sorry for the spirit. She told her that it would all be okay and that she should go toward the light. Mom said she didn't know if the ghost understood, but the smoky haze began to fade away and then it was gone.*

I asked the young woman if I could speak with her mother, but she was reluctant to give out her contact information. This was several years ago, and when I went back this year to ask again, I found she was no longer at the hotel.

A bartender at the Weatherford did agree to share her encounters with the paranormal for this book. Britt Jones is certain there is at least one ghostly presence that haunts the Zane Grey. Britt tends bar upstairs and says that the spirit of a woman makes herself known throughout the night. "I talk to her when it's not too busy, but if I get tied up with customers, pieces of ice start flying through the air. This spirit does not like being ignored."

Britt also shared several stories with NAU student Madison Easton, who wrote a paper on ghost hunting in Flagstaff in 2021: "During a closing shift, she [Britt] turned off the lights and locked all the doors to the third-story bar. No one could get in or out except for herself. When watching the security cameras, cloud-like figures passed across the screen and lingered. Unlike dust and unlike light. It was something unusual."

Jones also told Easton about sightings in the basement of a little girl who likes to duck under the pool table and disappear. These encounters freak out the bar patrons, who wonder if they've had way too much to drink.[15]

Drew Purcell, one of the hotel's managers, gave me a private tour of the building, which consisted of the labyrinth of rooms that make up the Weatherford. He allowed me a look behind locked doors on the upper floor as well as in the basement, including the remnants of a stone passageway. With my recorder on and camera filming, I poked about the most notorious rooms, while Drew relayed interesting bits of the building's history. It was late morning, and the Zane Grey bar was quiet, as was Charly's Pub and Grill downstairs. Drew shared several videos from his phone, including one from the week before of a beer bottle falling from its shelf inside Charly's. The bottle had been flush with the others and did appear to have a slight arc as it fell, as if it were "pushed." News of the flying bottle had already permeated the late-night Flagstaff crowd, and it was quite evocative. Purcell said he considers himself an open-minded skeptic, and the video is a rare piece of evidence he can't explain away.

We started the walk from Charly's, and Purcell took me through the lobby into the restaurant and back through the kitchen. We then proceeded downstairs into what is now the Gopher Hole Pub. This is the basement of the building and a section of it is locked to the public. Drew said that owners Sam Green and Henry Taylor had thoroughly researched the hotel's history in the decades since Taylor bought the Weatherford in 1975. The basement originally housed the kitchen for the restaurant upstairs. Behind a locked door on the west wall are several stone steps that were the beginnings of a passageway that led to the Majestic and later the Orpheum. This tunnel has been packed with dirt and rock and is now a door to nowhere, but it is proof the long-rumored passage existed.

Purcell confirmed the stories that owner Sam Green's dog would not go past an invisible line when the basement was just an unfinished workshop. We ran into Greg Green who, along with being head of maintenance for the past four decades, is also Sam's brother. He's been through the renovations and expansions and spoke independently about the basement area:

> *My sister's dog, Mona, was so loyal and well trained. That dog followed her everywhere around the hotel, because she and Henry lived here for a few years while they were renovating it. But when it came to the basement, the dog would not move past this part of the room. Sam would coax her and call her name, but the dog would just whimper and not move.*

I asked Greg if he had ever felt anyone or anything supernatural while he worked down here, and he replied, "Well, this is an old hotel. I've had some weird feelings when I've been here alone—but I've never seen a ghost or a spirit. But have I ever felt like something was here that I couldn't see… yes, probably."

The Taylors' daughter Chelsea had her own experiences in what is now the Gopher Hole, which I'll detail later in this chapter.

Drew and I left the basement pub and headed upstairs to the Zane Grey Ballroom. This large area has a fireplace and polished wood floors and manages to feel both spacious and cozy. There's a door that leads to the narrow balcony that runs along the outside of the hotel at the third-story level. The ballroom is connected to the bar by a few steps through an open doorway. Interestingly, the ballroom itself was once divided into a series of hotel rooms, and Zane Grey likely wrote some of his novels here. I've already detailed a few of the stories I've heard of hauntings in both the bar and ballroom. In October 2021, there were increased sightings of a ghostly woman who followed guests into the ladies' third-floor bathroom. Britt, the bartender, believes it's the same spirit that follows her around as she prepares drinks and has been known to throw ice at her head. The increased paranormal activity noted is thought by some to be due to activated spirits, happy that guests were finally returning after the Covid shutdown.

Purcell finished the third-floor tour by unlocking the door to the notorious room 54. We went inside what had once been two bedrooms and is now a combination laundry and storage area for hotel amenities. Drew said he was aware of the hauntings associated with it—the honeymoon couple, apparitions of a bride and groom, music coming from behind the locked door at 2:00 a.m.—but that he hasn't experienced anything paranormal up here. I asked if the current owners ever spoke about ghosts or spirits inhabiting the Weatherford:

> *Henry Taylor has owned the hotel since the 1970s, and both of them* [Green and Taylor] *lived here during the 1990s when they were personally doing a lot of the restoration. I get the feeling that they take the hotel as it is. It's a very old building with a lot of history, and if there are noises or lights or strange happenings—they say it's part of what they have grown to love and live with.*

After we had finished with the upstairs bar and ballroom, Purcell and I were standing on the landing above the lobby. There's an open office area

The Zane Grey Ballroom was once part of the hotel made up of guest rooms. Wispy spirits have been reported near the fireplace and dancing in the east corner, close to the window. *Author's collection.*

toward the corner with a desk and phone, where a young woman was busy at work. Drew had carefully closed and locked doors as we exited the various parts of the hotel, and we were talking casually before descending the stairs. As we turned to go, the door leading to the Zane Grey Ballroom slowly creaked open on its own. The three of us were surprised, and while Drew was uncertain if he had actually locked the door, he had definitely closed it. The door is solid, and when Purcell closed it again, it made a resounding *click*. The young woman at the desk smiled and raised her eyebrows before returning her attention to her call. It was the perfect ending to the walk through the Weatherford.

There is, however, one more person who has creepy tales to tell of the Weatherford's ghostly spirits. Chelsea is the daughter of Sam and Henry. During the 1990s, the hotel went through extensive remodeling thanks in part to a grant from the Heritage Fund. Green and Taylor took a hands-on approach to the renovations and essentially lived in a wing of the building while overseeing the work. Chelsea lived there as well and tells the story of befriending a "dark but not evil" entity that lived in the basement, whom she called Algernon. In a YouTube video titled "Haunted Weatherford Hotel," she speaks of some of the phenomena she has encountered:

> *When I'm wandering around, I'll hear some whispering and talking and whistling in my ears….I'm all alone in this big building, but then I realize someone else is here trying to let me know that they're here….When I was a little girl, my friend Cleo would be over* [in the basement]….*We'd hang out with an entity named Algernon. We'd bounce the ball back against the wall and talk about whatever children talk about.*

Chelsea goes on in the video to describe a medium named Margaret who was also aware of Algernon and was surprised that the then little girl was interacting with him so easily.

Hopefully there will be a lot more coming from the Weatherford on its YouTube channel. Drew also posted several cellphone images, including one of two shadowy arms with clawed hands reaching toward a pair of unsuspecting legs. Very creepy! The video of the falling beer bottle can also be viewed there, in "Haunted Weatherford Hotel, Part One."

I reviewed my own video and audio after the tour, checking for an EVP or any unexplained images. I found neither from this walk. Years ago, I was in the Zane Grey Ballroom, and as I was standing by the fireplace with a friend, I had the distinct feeling someone came up behind me. I quickly turned around, but no one was there, and the energy dissipated. Oddly, my friend had the same sense at the same time, and both of us felt chilled by the incident. That happened several years before I began to do a deep dive on the history and hauntings in town. Personally, I'm certain that the Weatherford is home to several spirits that are attached to the people who work there. Occasionally they may deign to show themselves to visitors and the rest of us. Like most spirits, they come out on their own timetable and not for our convenience.[16]

CHAPTER 5

DR. RAYMOND'S HOME AND OFFICE

A few blocks south of the Weatherford, tucked between shops on the west side of Leroux, is a charming New Mexico–style building. The front of the structure is taken up with two large windows and an arched entry with three steps leading to the front door. Made of red brick, it's unusually long and narrow with an interior that's divided into multiple small rooms with hardwood floors. Like many of the stores downtown, the building also has a full basement. This was the home and offices of one of Flagstaff's most beloved physicians, Dr. R.O. Raymond, who served the community from 1909 until sometime before his death in 1959.

Dr. Raymond was born in 1876 and graduated from medical school in St. Louis around 1904. He then headed west in search of the cool, dry air as so many victims of lung disease and arthritis did in those years. By the time he made his way to Flagstaff in 1909, he had regained his health and was ready to accept patients and establish a practice here. Platt Cline describes Dr. Raymond as "tall, slim, neat, always dressed in a three-piece suit with hat." He was frequently in the company of his beloved corgis as he made his way through town, checking on patients and bearing gifts of organic vegetables from his garden. Dr. Raymond never married, although there were rumors he had a paramour. He was described as an original thinker with an independent mindset. My favorite story about the doctor is that he was known to make house calls and gently chide his rougher patients about the dangers of too much whiskey and smoking. The fact that he did this yet remained so popular speaks volumes.[17]

This was the home and office of Dr. R.O. Raymond, Flagstaff's beloved family physician in the early 1900s. *Author's collection.*

Dr. Raymond was eighty-three when he died, and he left a real legacy to the town he loved. Over the course of his years, Raymond had amassed large tracts of land. He donated various parcels for recreational use and gave several acres for the site of the new hospital. He had also saved some money, which was interesting given the number of patients who left him with IOUs. Those funds went into the Raymond Education Foundation, which is still offering scholarships in 2022. Dr. Raymond is buried south of Flagstaff in Kachina Village, inside Raymond County Park. A rare picture of the man with his three sweet corgis is etched into a plaque outside the stone enclosure that contains his grave.

The building that was once Raymond's home and medical office has changed hands frequently in the past three decades. Speaking with a former occupant, the constant turnover has less to do with ghosts and more with Flagstaff's notoriously high rents. As of this writing, the building is once again empty. However, I spoke with several people who either worked in or operated a business from there and asked about any paranormal experiences.

Dr. Raymond was buried south of town in 1959 in an area that was once part of his Pump House Ranch. Today, Raymond County Park—where his tomb is located—is just outside Kachina Village. *Author's collection.*

One such woman took out a lease and opened a yoga studio/organic cooking business inside the house. Yoga classes were held downstairs in the finished basement, while she planned to hold the cooking lessons in the upstairs kitchen. I spoke to Theresa on a sunny afternoon as she was sweeping out the foyer. The doors and windows were open, creating a gentle cross breeze that naturally cooled the old home. There wasn't even a hint of the paranormal in the air that day. I asked her if she had seen or felt anything out of the ordinary as she readied the place for clients:

> *There is a benign presence—like a set of eyes watching me—that I've felt a couple of times since I rented the house. I know the stories about Dr. Raymond, so maybe that has influenced me. About a week ago, I was sweeping the back rooms and had the doors open, like today. I went through the front door to set the garbage outside, and when I turned to come back in, I saw the figure of a man at the back door. He was tall and thin and had an old-fashioned hat on, with a brim. I really couldn't make out his*

> *features, but I had the strong sense he was amused. Then he began to disintegrate—became just a wispy column of air.*

Theresa denied she felt afraid. "That was what was really weird—the whole thing felt normal and natural. I'm sure it was Dr. Raymond and he was coming by to see what's going on inside his old digs."

The building was empty for a year or so after the yoga studio closed. However, it wasn't long before Flagstaff General Store took out a lease and opened its eclectic doors to the public. Filled with the usual tourist paraphernalia, it also sold handcrafted clothing, home décor, lotions and potions and a few other items. In October 2019, I ventured inside and spoke to a young woman manning the cash register. I asked if she was aware of anything out of the ordinary happening in the store. From my notes, I've reconstructed what she said:

> *You mean paranormal, like ghosts? I've never seen anything, but there are a lot of stories about Dr. Raymond, who lived here and had his medical office in the house. One of the guys who works here said he felt like someone was following him around the basement when he was setting up displays. And sometimes I feel a presence in the back rooms—but it's a very nice, very comforting presence.*

The Flagstaff General Store lasted a few years in the building before relocating to east Aspen. The former home and office sits empty on its small parcel, awaiting a new owner.

A local psychic, who I'll identify only as "M.," agreed to meet at the Raymond Building one dark October evening in 2021. There were a few people in attendance as she circled the north side of the building, placing her hand against the exterior brick walls and working her way along. She came to the fenced backyard, where Raymond had tended to his organic vegetable garden, and stood in silence. As far as I know, this woman had limited knowledge of Dr. Raymond and his history with the town, but she noted, "I feel like there's a lot of blood and death associated with this house. I can't tell if it comes from the original owner or if a kind of secret activity took place inside. It feels like surgery or medical procedures took place inside the house, and a lot of pain was associated with it." The psychic concluded by saying it was difficult for her to get a reading from the outside looking in. M. also didn't tap into any feeling for the man himself or his corgis, which likely roamed the fenced yard.

The fenced backyard behind the Raymond Building was the site of the doctor's organic garden. Raymond was known to gift patients with his produce as he made rounds through town accompanied by his beloved corgis. *Author's collection.*

As for the psychic's impression of blood and death, it's possible patients were brought into the doctor's house and passed there. It's also true that in the early 1900s, many doctors removed tonsils and performed minor surgeries in their offices. Dr. Raymond was likely no different. Men from the lumber mill were among his patients, and some of them suffered horrific injuries. A doctor from that era would have treated all sorts of human ailments and illnesses. However, Flagstaff had at least one hospital at the time for patients with catastrophic illnesses or injuries and it's doubtful Raymond's office was any kind of trauma center.

What struck me that night was how differently M. and I experienced the old home. The times I'd walked through and explored the building, I felt an air of excitement about the place. Its beautiful hardwood floors, large windows and all the nooks and crannies—to me, it felt eclectic. Yet M. was immediately on guard as she walked around the building's perimeter. To her, the place emitted vibrations of pain and suffering to the extent she said she didn't have a feel for Raymond himself. To this date, we've been

Looking inside the arched front windows of the Raymond Building. Toward the back of the house, there are many small rooms, indicative of a doctor's office. *Author's collection.*

unable to do a proper investigation inside; however, it's certainly deserving of one and is on the list.

When Raymond died, his body was placed in a pine box and driven south of Flagstaff about four miles to Pump House Wash. Doc loved this area and he had specifically chosen it for his final resting place. According to Platt Cline, the funeral was attended by hundreds of townsfolk, including many from the Basque community. Dr. Raymond had forged a special bond with these sheepherders from the Pyrenees Mountain region and in his later years would follow them south in the winter. They, in turn, had great affection for the doctor and turned out en masse to pay their respects. As mentioned earlier, Raymond surprised everyone by the large amount of wealth he had accumulated over the years, most of which he left to the community trust.

CHAPTER 6
THE RAILROAD DEPOT

Anyone exploring the history and/or hauntings of Flagstaff must give serious consideration to the town's train station, which sits just north of the tracks on Route 66. Travelers on Amtrak's east–west route—the Southwest Chief—depart and arrive weekly and often crowd the small waiting room inside. Upstairs, the building's rooms once served as offices for the Flagstaff Visitors' Center. Although it has been through several renovations, the train station is basically the same as when it opened in 1926.

As written elsewhere in this book, the Atlantic and Pacific Railway was vital to Flagstaff's growth and stability. The first depot was an old wooden boxcar that sat beside the tracks, close to where the station is today. A few years later another boxcar was added, and then another. The townspeople lobbied for a more permanent structure, and soon a beautiful sandstone building was constructed. That building, which the town quickly outgrew, sits just west of the current depot and houses the offices of the chamber of commerce. The current station is situated on the south side of town, being located south of historic Route 66. It remains at the center of Flagstaff's commerce and tourism, bringing together the university community with the historic downtown district.

It's believed the hauntings reported inside the depot grew out of the tracks that run alongside it. In the 1880s, these rails were laid with the blood, sweat and tears of the gandy dancers and other laborers. In the decades following, accidents were not uncommon along the tracks, as human error caused derailments, switching problems and all forms of

Approaching the Flagstaff train depot from the east. The tracks that run alongside have been the site of countless accidents and suicides throughout the decades. *Author's collection.*

collisions. Working for the railroad might have sounded romantic and prestigious, but it was also very dangerous.

One of the most enduring tales of a ghostly sighting involves a brakeman who was killed in the early 1900s. While not specifically named, the story may have grown out of the untimely death of Leo Bart. Leo was a popular young man in Flagstaff who worked as a brakeman for the railroad. In 1926, he was riding the line near Canyon Diablo, lantern in hand and standing on the running board of the train. It was his duty to throw open the switch at the appropriate time. Leo was riding with engine no. 1673; around the bend, the no. 10 train was approaching. As the no. 10 roared past, it somehow caught hold of Leo Bart and took his head with it down the track. The young man was the sole support of his mother and sisters, and the whole town mourned his loss. Leo Bart was buried in Calvary Catholic Cemetery, but his story was not forgotten.[18]

Through the decades, reports of blinking lights that disappear into the darkness have been recounted by locals. These white flashes are seen along the tracks and are said to resemble lantern signals. Young Leo was killed several miles east of Flagstaff; however, his story was all too common during the railroad's heyday. The *Coconino Sun* has many accounts of brakemen and rail workers cut down in their prime while working on the line. To this day, the flashing lights seen along the tracks that suddenly disappear are thought to be their ghostly signals from the past.

Reports of paranormal activity inside the depot have been more recent and became so prevalent in the early 2000s that a psychic was brought into the building and asked his impressions. According to an October 13, 2009 article in the *Daily Sun*, employee Justin Connors said the psychic found "about 29 spirits in the depot." "A colleague was down here getting some product, Connors explained....She saw what appeared to be a spirit... dressed up in an old-style conductor's outfit. They locked eyes....The train went by, he [the spirit] ran by and went up the stairs. She thinks he was trying to catch up with the train."

The same article contained a report of trash cans that rose up from the floor and then slammed down again. Another incident was that of a laptop that flew across the waiting room after a visitor disavowed the idea of ghosts. According to employees at the time, the phenomena were of such an angry nature that there was growing concern someone would be injured.[19]

Reports of supernatural encounters and strange phenomena have persisted through the years. People who work inside the depot today have stories of footsteps heard climbing the stairs and lights turning on and off by themselves. Some have seen shadow figures darting across the rooms and others have heard someone walking about the otherwise empty depot after hours.

As with many of Flagstaff's buildings, some areas inside the train depot have been repurposed over the years. On a clear November morning in 2021, Joshua Hudlow, an employee of the visitors' center, took me on a tour of the building. It had been years since I'd been inside the depot, and I had a chance to look around before our appointment. It was a pleasantly busy day, with tourists perusing the gift shop and seeking information on what to do in town. The station's ground floor is basically divided into two large rooms. Amtrak's waiting room is to the east and looks like any small depot area, with a ticket window and wooden benches. The short hall to the west opens into the gift shop, filled with books, postcards, candy, clothing—everything and anything Flagstaff. The door leading to the upstairs room and the one to the basement were locked.

Taking a break, Josh showed me a few improvements to the main floor before we went outside to access the upstairs. In 2021, it was being used to store odds and ends. The room is large and open, has a bathroom in the corner and is rather dark, even after the lights are flipped on. Twenty-odd years ago, it was used by various groups that approached the city looking for a space in which to meet. SCORE held monthly work sessions in the room, and groups such as AA would hold weekly or biweekly meetups. Josh said he occasionally finds himself with work to do up here and this is where he's had one paranormal experience:

> *I was upstairs—either getting something from one of the boxes or putting something together—when I had to use the bathroom. I don't always lock the door at the bottom of the stairs, so when I heard footsteps walking across the cement floor, I thought someone had come in from the sidewalk. The bathroom door was closed, but the footsteps were walking across the room toward me, so I yelled out, "I'm in here" so whoever it was would know. The footsteps stopped outside the bathroom door, but no one answered. That was pretty weird, so I hurried and opened the door—but no one was up here. I know what I heard—and there wasn't enough time for anyone to walk across the room to the bathroom then leave before I opened the door.*

Josh said that he has heard footsteps upstairs more than once, and while he's had "feelings" of a presence in the depot, that's his most solid experience. Interestingly, I took a dozen pictures upstairs that should have easily saved to my camera, but they ended up lost from that visit.

Returning to the gift shop, Josh unlocked the nondescript door that leads to the basement. We made our way down the narrow steps into an area that many paranormal investigators have tagged the building's hotspot. This space is used for storage by the visitors' center and contains boxes of seasonal decorations as well as extra merchandise stacked on wire shelves. The basement has a dark, dank feel to it with cement walls and narrow, wood-framed windows with frosted glass. This part of the depot sits below street level now and—like other buildings and roads south of the tracks—has experienced flooding in the past. It's also the area where the employee encountered the apparition of a train conductor. Strange phenomena occur down here to this day, according to the people who work inside.

Josh told me a story about an eerie incident that happened to a coworker several years ago. She was down in the basement folding T-shirts and taking stock of inventory. She went back up the stairs to return to the gift shop but found the door to the shop was locked from the outside. This was highly improbable, as she'd left it unlocked and no one else was in the depot. The

Right: These are the steps leading down into the station's basement. It's down here that employees have encountered apparitions and experienced paranormal phenomena. *Author's collection.*

Below: The basement is currently used to store seasonal decorations as well as extra merchandise sold in the depot's gift shop. *Author's collection.*

It was in this area that a former employee encountered a ghost thought to be a conductor. Another woman claimed she was locked in the basement by an unknown spirit while working down here. *Author's collection.*

woman said she had a strong feeling that the incident was precipitated by the spirit of a man who did not want her to leave the area. Trapped in the basement, she continued sorting through the merchandise for another half hour. When she tried the door again, it was unlocked.

Another employee, Lisa, has been with the visitors' center since 2021. She is Native American, and belief in spirits and the afterworld is part of her culture. She told me that while she's never been afraid at work, she has been aware of a spirit in the building:

> *I noticed the presence when I first started and…told them I was only there to work and not to harm them in any way and that I was sorry that they were there for whatever reason. Their presence was strong just before the* Dead Files *came* [October–November 2021], *and I felt they knew someone would be seeking them out. We had items in the gift shop in disarray every morning…items in places away from where they were normally…or upside down.*

Lisa then explained one of her cultural beliefs, Hopi quiet time:

> *Then in December during Hopi quiet time—this time is set aside for them* [spirits] *to roam the earth again—I was uneasy but...I said a prayer to let them know that only I knew it was their time to roam and to please not hurt any of the workers or people who came to the visitors' center because they did not know or understand. When I say quiet time, we give Mother Earth that time to rest (basically time off) since she is the one who watches over us all year trying to protect everyone from death.... We try not to disturb the ground or be loud, like banging or digging.*

Lisa followed up that email with another, writing, "We teach our children to stay inside and be reverent and always show Mother Earth respect by giving her that time of rest." I found Lisa's story, and how it reflects the Hopi culture, both lovely and refreshing. I have to imagine she has assuaged many ghostly animosities in the depot.

It's a poorly kept secret in town that the tracks that run through Flagstaff have been a popular site for "death by train." When employees of the railroad get together outside work, the talk often turns to the grim topic of the latest suicide. Few people realize that these employees are the ones who are tasked with cleaning up the track after an accident is investigated. From conversations I've had with them, it's apparent there's a high level of stress and substance use among those who deal with the aftermath. As far as this book is concerned, I've wondered whether the flickering lights, shadow figures and strange sounds reported along the tracks are related more to the deaths in the past fifty years than those in the early 1900s.[20]

CHAPTER 7
THE HOTEL MONTE VISTA

Opinions vary as to what era was the most important in distinguishing Flagstaff as a town with its own eclectic flavor. However, no one could deny that the years 1933 through 1944 were among the most prolific in the city's history. According to multiple sources, the town made it through the Great Depression relatively unscathed. Thanks to an infusion of federal dollars for roadwork and rebuilding, by 1933 the town was facing the future with well-placed confidence. Tourism continued to rank in the top three industries fueling the economy, and the Hotel Monte V sat squarely in the center of the action.

Opening on January 1, 1927, the Monte Vista was seen as an alternative to the Weatherford. While hardly shabby, the older hotel was no longer considered as modern and luxurious as the citizens thought befitted the growing town. The Monte V was built by public funds and donations, with Zane Grey investing a large portion of the initial $200,000. The hotel's website states that it was the longest publicly held commercial property in Arizona until 1960. With four stories, seventy-three rooms and a (reputedly) haunted basement, it served as much more than a haven for visitors. Flagstaff businessmen and chamber officials had offices in the building, and the town's post office was once located inside. As the town began to regain its momentum in the mid-1930s, Hollywood returned—and one of its favorite staging areas was the Hotel Monte V.[21]

Former newspaper editor and historian Platt Cline did a wonderful job describing the people and events that shaped this city. He also wrote about the

Rooms 305 and 306 of the Monte V are visible from across San Francisco Street. Both rooms are associated with the paranormal and are popular with ghost hunters. *Author's collection.*

more obscure and colorful turns in the town's past that many had forgotten. Cline's book, *Mountain Town*, tells how Flagstaff just missed its chance to become the nation's Hollywood. Taken from an interview in the *Coconino Sun*, Cline wrote that Jesse L. Lasky and Cecil B. DeMille rode into town in 1912 to produce the movie *The Squaw Man*. On paper, Flagstaff seemed like an ideal place to permanently locate their new studio, the Jesse L. Lasky Feature Film Company. However, Lasky said when they arrived in town to begin the shoot, the weather turned cold and rainy. A snowstorm followed, which delayed the filming even further. Finally, a long-running battle in the area between the sheepherders and the cattlemen gave the directors second thoughts. The two men decided to continue westward with the film crew to Los Angeles, and the rest is movie history.[22]

Although none of the major studios put down roots in Northern Arizona, many continued to use the area to film the popular westerns of the day. The Monte Vista became the place to meet, eat and often sleep as the various production teams arrived in town. One prominent local, Lee Doyle, was in great demand by the moviemakers. He had the connections to procure the horses and authentic costumes that the studios needed. He was also well respected by several tribes in the area and would mediate between the Native American extras and the filmmakers. According to the *Sun*, Doyle was often found at the Monte V, mixing it up with both Hollywood types and the politicians and businesspeople who gathered there.

The Hotel Monte Vista has an extensive website where it lists famous guests who have stayed here. Not all the names are pulled from the annals of history. Along with Bob Hope and John Wayne, Michael J. Fox and Michael Stipe have spent the night in the hotel's beds. The website also has a page for reported hauntings, and some of these stories have become Flagstaff legends. I've found independent accounts that support a couple of the favorites listed there, which I'll explore along with the other paranormal encounters I've been told of.

One of the Monte V's most popular hauntings is that of the phantom bellboy. This sighting is linked to movie legend John Wayne, who purportedly had an encounter with the ghost while staying in room 210. The story goes as follows:

> *The Hotel Monte V was a favorite with the movie crowd, and many of the stars stayed in Flagstaff when filming on the Reservation. One evening, Wayne came back to the hotel and told the front desk he intended to go right to bed and did not want to be disturbed. He was comfortably ensconced in his room when, some thirty minutes later, there was a knock at his door. The movie star was reportedly irritated at the intrusion and yelled out, "Who is it?" When the voice replied, "Room service," he angrily strode to the door and threw it open, only to find...nothing. There was no one at the door or in the hallway or anywhere near the great man's room. When he called down to the front desk, the employee who answered was as puzzled as Wayne. No one from the restaurant or kitchen had been dispatched to room 210. This ghostly intrusion repeated itself several times during his stay, and Wayne was said to have thrown up his hands in surrender and learned to ignore the knocking.*

Left: The front desk has received phone calls from frightened guests complaining of strange noises and being touched by unseen hands. Going up the steps at the far end takes you to the meat man's wing. *Author's collection.*

Right: These steps, to the left of the San Francisco entrance, take the guest to the floor where John Wayne reported the phantom bellboy. *Author's collection.*

Another popular story of paranormal hijinks, based in historical reality, occurred in room 306. Prostitution in Flagstaff, while not exactly legal, was tolerated, taxed and licensed. It's been said that the good women in town turned a blind eye toward the activity south of the tracks but put their collective foot down when it came to gambling. It's one thing to toy with someone's affection but quite another to take away the family's hard-earned money. The paranormal activity in 306 has to do with the horrific deaths of two ladies of the evening that went unavenged.[23]

According to the hotel's website, the tragedy occurred in the 1940s. Two businessmen were in town, and as day turned to night, they went in search of female companionship. The men found two women who were willing and brought them back to room 306. The party was going well, with drinking and laughter, when something was said and the mood turned ugly. Loud arguing ensued and accusations flew, and then one of the men pushed his female guest out of the third-floor window. Before anyone on the street below could react, the second woman came tumbling out after her. Both women were badly injured and eventually died from the fall; the two men were never prosecuted.

I've spoken with several locals who have booked the room and came away with a tale to tell. Nick said he stayed there a few years ago with a friend after a night of drinking. He was startled awake in the early hours of the morning by a feeling of being suffocated:

> *I was in my mid-twenties then and in pretty good shape—if I hadn't been, I might have thought I was having a heart attack. It was very strange—I distinctly felt something or somebody outside of me pressing down on my throat and chest. I couldn't breathe, and I panicked. I jumped up—no one else was in the room but my friend in the next bed. And for a few seconds I really felt like someone was standing a few feet away, facing me. But, like I said, no one was there.*

Nick said the incident frightened him, but after walking the room and drinking water, he settled down and went back to sleep. Later that morning, when checking out, the front desk clerk asked him if he had any run-ins with the ladies of the night:

> *She* [the clerk] *was just kidding around—I know she didn't expect my reaction! The memory of what happened came rushing back, and I told her what I'd felt. She listened and laughed a bit—I think she could tell I was getting upset just remembering it. But she told me that there were a lot of guys who would wake up in 306 feeling like they were being strangled. Not the girlfriends or wives—just the guys. It's made me a believer in some kind of supernatural force that exists and that I can't explain.*

The desk clerk I spoke with reiterated Nick's story about 306 and added that room 305 also has its fair share of reported hauntings. According to the Monte V's website, room 305 was inhabited in the early 1970s by an elderly woman who moved into the hotel after her husband died. She enjoyed sitting in her rocking chair by the window, looking out on the street below. The widow eventually passed, and the hotel came into possession of her chair. According to both the clerk and the website, many guests in 305 report paranormal activity during the night. This particular chair has been seen rocking on its own, and some guests find it has moved from one part of the room to another. The closet inside 305 is also a source of some eerie phenomena. Visitors staying overnight have heard rapping and knocking sounds coming from within and a few have reported losing articles of clothing. A local woman who worked at the Monte V said that the scent of lilacs and/or lilies frequently wafts through room 305, without a detectable source.

One of the hotel's bars, the Rendezvous, was closed during the latter half of 2020 and well into 2021 due to Covid. Prior to the pandemic, the Rendezvous was among the most popular bars downtown, and plenty of stories of eerie and supernatural encounters have originated there. I spoke to a bartender in 2018 about tales repeated in town of a haunted jukebox, disappearing drinks and a ghostly couple dancing in the corner of the bar. She told me what she had experienced, as well as some of the stories told to her by co-workers:

> *I've worked in the hotel for a few years—not always at the Rendezvous—and I can tell you some of the stories are true. I've never seen the dancing couple, and I don't know about the jukebox. It's kind of touchy, and sometimes it plays a song that the customer says they didn't pick. I will tell you that the basement is haunted as...any other place in town. The owner stores bottles of alcohol down there, and if we're running low, one of us has to go downstairs and get a new one. I hate going down in the basement! I've heard voices down there—when no one else is there but me—and yes, I've heard the baby crying too. Whenever I go into the basement, I try and make it fast....When I turn to come back up the stairs, I feel like there's a pair of eyes standing at the bottom step, watching me run back up.*

The tale of the crying baby is so prevalent it made it onto the Monte V's website. It's been reported by hotel and bar personnel throughout the years, but there's no history or context in which to make sense of it. As far as anyone knows, there's never been a missing or murdered infant associated with the hotel. However, the unmistakable sound of an infant crying has reportedly been heard in the basement for decades. The same bartender told me that another employee was given permission to sleep downstairs for a few nights when his apartment needed emergency repairs. "He didn't last long down there—one night, I think. He said it was the creepiest place he's ever tried to sleep in...and it felt like someone was down there with him. He said he heard the baby crying too—no baby down there though."

Another entity said to haunt the basement is that of a shadow man. He's described as tall and unfriendly, and he makes his presence known to the workers who descend into his realm. The hotel's website alludes to the tunnel system that once ran beneath most of downtown Flagstaff. The tunnels have been sealed and the entryways blocked with dirt and cement for a few decades. However, there are locals who believe these shadow entities still live in the underground passageways and easily pass into the buildings that were once connected. There's a surprising number of encounters by employees who are just doing their job when they're frightened by an unhappy spirit.

Another little-known fact is that Flagstaff Undertaking Parlors was once located just east of the Monte Vista in what is now its parking lot. Whether the mortuary's proximity to the hotel is related to some of the paranormal experiences reported—and whether the basement entities are related to the mortuary—is up for speculation. However, over the decades and especially during the flu epidemic of 1920, many infants and children died in town. Their remains would have been taken to the parlor and prepared before burial in Citizens Cemetery.

There are a few other spirits said to roam the halls of the Hotel Monte V. One of the local favorites is that of the meat man who's said to haunt room 220. Online reviews testify to paranormal phenomena that occur

The south side and back lot of the Monte V as seen from Aspen. The door into the hotel bar, the Rendezvous, is here. This parking lot was once the site of Flagstaff Undertaking Parlors. *Author's collection.*

in the room, especially to those who throw out insults and taunts before turning in. The meat man was a local butcher who became a long-term renter at the hotel. Evidently, he thought it would be cheaper to bring his work "home" with him instead of renting shop space. The man would hang beef and venison from the chandelier in 220's ceiling and then carve and package the cuts of meat. The problem arose when he suddenly passed away. It was several days before the stench of decaying flesh permeated the hotel floor and his body was discovered. After what must have been a horrific clean-up job, room 220 was ready to be rented again. However, complaints began to come from 220's guests—especially females—that they were unable to sleep through the night. They were awakened by strange laughter and murmuring voices, and some said they felt threatened by an invisible presence. Through the years, maintenance people have reported puzzling electrical disturbances with the lights, radios and televisions in room 220. Ghost hunters who have conducted investigations of the hotel often point to the second floor as being trolled by an unhappy entity, and locals pin this disturbance on the meat man.

CHAPTER 8

THE OLD WALKUP HOUSE

The Flagstaff of 1937 had grown by leaps and bounds from the town that existed just ten years earlier. After emerging from the Great Depression, the people kept their eyes toward the future, and it paid off. The lumber mills were turning out wood products, Lowell Observatory played host to astronomers from all over the world and the Teachers College (now NAU) boasted a healthy enrollment. That spring, Flagstaff was bustling with excitement and preparing for the festivals and conventions slated for the summer. The town was geographically set apart but was becoming more accessible—and there was a lot going on that year.[24]

James D. Walkup was one of the more prominent men around town in the mid-1930s. J.D., as he was known, was a Tennessean who came to the mountain around 1920 after being gassed in World War I. In 1937, Walkup was the chairman of the Coconino County Board of Supervisors and secretary of the chamber of commerce. His name was frequently mentioned in the town's weekly newspaper, the *Coconino Sun*. The thirty-seven-year-old lived with his wife, Marie, and their four children in a large, comfortable home at the north end of Leroux. The house was just a few blocks from the heart of downtown, where J.D. maintained an office in the Hotel Monte Vista.

On a cool summer's evening in July 1937, a horrific scene began to unfold inside the Walkups' two-story home. The tragedy ended several hours later and four miles north of town at the Flagstaff Country Club. This sad event was detailed in the book *Flagstaff's Walkup Family Murders: A Shocking 1937 Tragedy*. Those hearing the story today are disturbed not only

In 1937, the Walkup house on North Leroux was the site of one of Flagstaff's saddest and most horrific tragedies. *Author's collection.*

by the crime but also by how little information is available on the family. What follows is a shortened account of that night and the hauntings that are reported even today.

July 22, 1937, was a lovely summer's day in this small town of five thousand. That Thursday, J.D. Walkup awoke and readied himself to drive the long, winding route to Phoenix for another meeting, this one regarding the state tax commission. His departure was timed to the afternoon after he was asked to take several members of the Flagstaff girls' softball team along. The team had earned a spot in the Western States Softball tournament, with a game scheduled to be played Friday in Phoenix. There was nothing nefarious or unusual in the request to carpool. While people today can drive the 140 miles between the two cities in a few hours, there was no direct route in the 1930s. The five-hour journey through canyonlands and national forests, up mountains and across high desert plateaus was stunning but primitive. *Most* of the backroads are at least paved now, although the switchbacks remain daunting to some. In 1937, those making the drive between the two cities often carried other passengers.

Not much is known about what happened in Flagstaff after J.D. kissed Marie and the children goodbye that afternoon. There are reports that the older children—Daniel, age ten; Rose, eight; and John, four—were seen outside playing until early evening. Baby Elizabeth, twenty months old, was seen in the late afternoon by an unnamed person, as was her mother. Marie had called Dr. Fronske the afternoon before, complaining of a stomach ailment and concerned that the children may have caught it. Fronske later intimated that he thought Mrs. Walkup's complaints were largely unfounded. In any event, the children felt well enough to be outside, possibly playing tag in their large front yard.

Sometime around 10:30 p.m. that Thursday, the telephone in the Fronske residence rang. The doctor and his wife were gone for the evening, and the eldest Fronske son, Robert, was left in charge of his siblings and of taking any messages. As reported the following day in the *Coconino Sun*, when he picked up the phone that evening, Marie Walkup's voice was on the other end:

> *"Is this Dr. Fronske's residence?" she asked.*
> *"Yes," Robert told her.*
> *"Oh, don't call him," she said. "Just take this message."*
> *Robert had her wait until he got a pencil, when she said:*
> *"Please have Dr. Fronske call at the house on his early round of visits."*
> *Then, after a moment, she said:*
> *"Wait a minute—Be sure to tell him not tonight, but tomorrow morning."*

A few hours later, just after midnight, two young couples were ending a moonlit stroll through the quiet, wooded area surrounding the Flagstaff Country Club. The four had been enjoying the stars and passing a small flask between them, giggling over this harmless bit of trespassing around the golf course. As the group rounded a corner near the first hole, they stopped short at the sight of a car on the frontage road. It sat in silence, silhouetted in the light cast by the evening's full moon. When no one emerged from the shadows to challenge their presence, the four moved slowly toward the vehicle. As they continued their approach, it was clear no one was inside, although the driver's door appeared to be slightly ajar. Rounding the back of the car, one of the girls let out a scream, causing the others to rush to her side. There they were greeted by a particularly gruesome sight that would stick in their minds for years to come. Lying on the ground, clothed only in a nightgown saturated with blood, was the body of a young woman. Her face appeared undamaged, but the gaping hole in her chest and an old army rifle off to her side told a story that would soon be plastered across the *Sun*. The dead woman's right foot was bare, with the errant slipper laying close to her body.

What followed was the first of many journeys that night between the sheriff's office and the country club, which was located about four miles north of town. Even today, eighty-five years later, the area seems isolated and unusually dark at night despite the expansive, star-filled sky. When one remembers that there were no cellphones—indeed, Dr. Fronske had only recently installed a home phone—it helps in appreciating the difficult logistics those involved were faced with. This became increasingly true as the horror of the night continued to unfold.

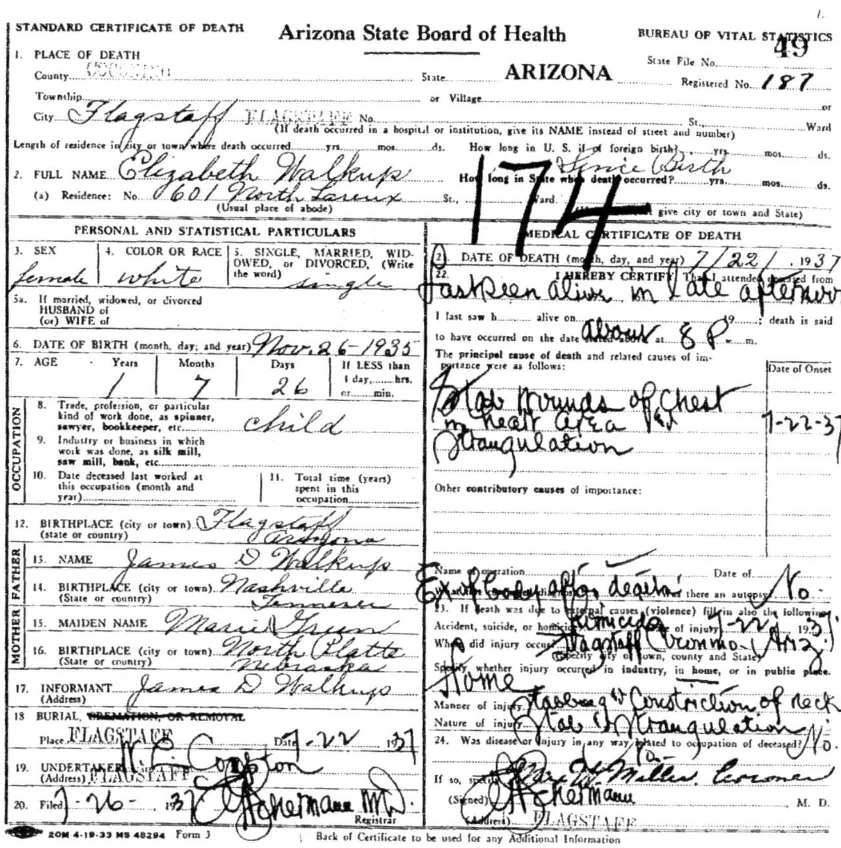

STANDARD CERTIFICATE OF DEATH — Arizona State Board of Health — BUREAU OF VITAL STATISTICS

State File No. 49 — Registered No. 187 — ARIZONA

1. PLACE OF DEATH — City: Flagstaff

2. FULL NAME: Elizabeth Walkups — How long in State: Since Birth

(a) Residence: No. 601 North Leroux

174

PERSONAL AND STATISTICAL PARTICULARS

3. SEX: female — 4. COLOR OR RACE: white — 5. SINGLE, MARRIED, WIDOWED, or DIVORCED: single

6. DATE OF BIRTH: Nov. 26-1935

7. AGE: 1 Years, 7 Months, 26 Days

8. Trade, profession, or particular kind of work done: child

12. BIRTHPLACE: Flagstaff, Arizona

13. NAME (Father): James D. Walkups

14. BIRTHPLACE: Nashville, Tennessee

15. MAIDEN NAME (Mother): Marie Green

16. BIRTHPLACE: North Platte, Nebraska

17. INFORMANT: James D. Walkups

18. BURIAL — Place: FLAGSTAFF — Date: 7-22 1937

19. UNDERTAKER: N. C. Compton — FLAGSTAFF

20. Filed: 7-26-1937 — Ackermann M.D., Registrar

MEDICAL CERTIFICATE OF DEATH

21. DATE OF DEATH: 7/22/1937

22. Last seen alive in late afternoon — death is said to have occurred about 8 P.M.

The principal cause of death: Stab wounds of chest in heart area; Strangulation — Date of Onset: 7-22-37

Ex. of body after death — Was there an autopsy? No

23. Homicide — Date of injury: 7-22-1937 — Where did injury occur: Flagstaff, Coconino, Ariz. — Home

Manner of injury: Stabbing & Constriction of neck — Nature of injury: Stab & Strangulation

24. Was disease or injury related to occupation of deceased? No

(Signed) Ackermann, M.D. — Fred W. Miller, Coroner — FLAGSTAFF

20M 4-19-33 MS 48294 Form 3 — Back of Certificate to be used for any Additional Information

Elizabeth Walkup, nicknamed Phoebe by her elder siblings, was last seen alive on the afternoon of July 22. She was found strangled in her crib and had a stab wound to her chest. *Courtesy of Karen Renner.*

After returning to town and dropping off his friends, twenty-nine-year-old Ed Conrad went to the sheriff's office to inform the deputy that a dead body had been found near the golf course. Deputy Francis gathered reinforcements and returned to the club with Conrad in tow. As they approached, the men recognized the Walkup vehicle sitting silently where the young trespassers had last seen it. As they pulled alongside, the two deputies were able to identify the woman lying on the ground—it was Marie Walkup.

Deputy Francis took charge, leaving his partner and young Conrad at the scene as he drove back to town to gather a coroner's jury. While he made the necessary phone calls and waited for the men's arrival (it was about 1:00 a.m.), he turned over the night's events in his mind. Flagstaff in 1937 was a town of five thousand, and the sheriff's office had a bead on most people's whereabouts. Francis knew that J.D. had left that afternoon for Phoenix and was expected to be gone for several days. That being true, and with Marie lying dead beside the family car, who was watching the four Walkup children? Francis decided to stop by the house on the way back to the country club and make provisions for their care until J.D. could arrive and take over.

However, the deputy's concern for the welfare of the Walkup children proved to be unnecessary. Accompanied by the county coroner and two other officials, he drove the short distance to the home on Leroux. It was 1:30 a.m., and both the house and surrounding neighborhood sat in stillness. As the four men climbed the steps to the front door, they noticed a note tacked to the outside. Unfolding the piece of white paper, they read the simple words: "Dr. Fronske, step into the bedrooms." On the porch next to the door sat an empty milk bottle with another piece of paper, this one furled and stuck inside the jar's mouth. Opening it, they read the words: "No milk today."

Two of the men left to notify Fronske while Francis and the remaining official tried the front door. It was unlocked, and they decided to look inside, confining their search to the first floor. The home was deathly still, but nothing appeared out of order. The kitchen and dining area were free of clutter, and nothing looked out of place in the living room. They crossed to the back of the house, where a long hallway with two bedrooms at either end finished the first floor. Opening the door to the right, the men stepped inside a child's bedroom.

The room contained both a crib and a regular bed, and the men first checked on twenty-month-old Elizabeth. The toddler appeared to be asleep, with a clean blanket covering her body and a little teddy bear tucked under her chin. It was only upon closer inspection that Francis noticed she wasn't breathing. Pulling the covers aside, neither man detected obvious signs of trauma. However, when one of them removed the stuffed bear, an angry circle of welts on Elizabeth's neck became visible. A quick check of the other bed, which contained the eldest child, Daniel, revealed much the same.

Shaken, the two men beat a hasty exit and waited for Dr. Fronske on the porch. When he arrived, accompanied by the remainder of the coroner's jury, he was given a rundown on the findings downstairs. Dr. Fronske never spoke publicly about the horrors he encountered that night in the Walkup house. As the family physician, he had been inside the home many times before. As he climbed the stairs to the second-story bedroom, he must have dreaded what he knew awaited him. The upstairs room where John and Rose slept was dark and quiet, and to the casual observer, the two children appeared to be deeply asleep. Like their siblings, both had been bathed and dressed in clean pajamas, with fresh sheets pulled up to their chins. It was only by pulling down the covers and inspecting each child's neck that Fronske saw the marks of strangulation. After his examination, Fronske formally declared all four children deceased, killed at the hands of their mother. Flagstaff Undertaking Parlor was called to take the bodies.

The events of that night shook the small mountain town to its core. People surrounded the grieving husband and father, while notes of condolence and flower arrangements poured in. The five members of the Walkup family were buried in a single, double-wide plot in Citizens Cemetery the following Monday. Afterward, there was no public comment, no newspaper mentions of Marie and her children. It was as if they had never existed.

There have been several hauntings reported in and around the house on Leroux. However, it's worth mentioning the unanswered questions about the Walkup family. Who was Marie Walkup, and what could have been so wrong in her life that this tragedy unfolded? How could Flagstaff bury the memory of this once prominent family so efficiently that, until quite recently, they were unknown? While these aspects of the tragedy were explored in the book *Flagstaff's Walkup Family Murders*, much is still open to speculation.

The man who currently resides in the Leroux house has a connection to it that goes back to the time of the murders. Steve Rawlinson said his grandparents bought the house from J.D. himself when the bereaved man could no longer face the emptiness there. Steve implied several times (usually with a laugh) that he is too thick-headed to believe in spirits. "I've never seen anything frightening or supernatural in all the years I've lived here." However, he did concede that his daughter Megan, who was raised in the home, reported several encounters when she was a child. I was fortunate enough to sit down with Megan on a rainy October evening, and the stories she shared were both exciting and disturbing.[25]

A vivacious young mother in her early thirties who now has a home of her own, Megan described a childhood sometimes filled with terror. While nighttime was the worst, she said that even during the day, the house could suddenly exhibit chaotic, supernatural energies. As we sat talking, she described some of the phenomena that went on inside:

> *Growing up in my house, I didn't know anything about that stuff* [the Walkup murders]*....It was nearly impossible for me to sleep at night....I slept upstairs in the far room, the back room, and when we were very young, my brother and I shared a bedroom....He* [Megan's brother] *said he never heard anything, but for me, it was very chaotic at night. It sounded like someone was running up and down the stairs—almost every night! And then I'd hear voices, but I couldn't tell what they were saying. It was like a low muttering or mumbling on the other side of the room....There's this closet upstairs, and inside of it—that's where we kept our toys....But the sounds of the toys that I heard* [at night] *were not like the sound of the toys we had.... There was a ringing of a tricycle bell and the sounds of a train set, but we didn't own a train set or a bicycle with that bell....But it was the sound of footsteps running up and down the stairs that really terrified me.*

Megan also described an old stairwell that was behind a door near the upstairs toy closet that opened to a set of narrow stairs:

> *It was like a steep, narrow drop to the outside....It was always very dark inside, and my parents would shove furniture against it. When I was a toddler, they put my crib there, and I have deep, vivid memories of being in that crib and being terrified....I spent so much of my childhood unable to sleep and terrified of my bedroom and not knowing why.*

Megan also described slamming doors and kitchen cabinets opening and closing on their own. Despite all that, neither her father nor mother seemed aware of the chaos that befell the house at night. It wasn't until she was ten or so, when her father rented out the house to a young woman for a year, that Megan learned of the tragedy that unfolded within its walls.

> *The woman who rented our house began experiencing strange things, and so she started doing some research. Somewhere she came across the story of*

STANDARD CERTIFICATE OF DEATH
Arizona State Board of Health
BUREAU OF VITAL STATISTICS

1. PLACE OF DEATH
County COCONINO State ARIZONA State File No. 51 Registered No. 183
Township or Village
City Flagstaff Arizona No. St. Ward
(If death occurred in a hospital or institution, give its NAME instead of street and number)
Length of residence in city or town where death occurred 22 yrs. mos. ds. How long in U.S., if of foreign birth? yrs. mos. ds.
2. FULL NAME Marie (Green) Walkup
(a) Residence: No. 601 North LaRoux St. How long in State where death occurred? 22 yrs. mos. ds.
(Usual place of abode) (If non-resident give city or town and State)

167

PERSONAL AND STATISTICAL PARTICULARS
3. SEX female
4. COLOR OR RACE white
5. SINGLE, MARRIED, WIDOWED, or DIVORCED (Write the word) married
5a. If married, widowed, or divorced HUSBAND of (or) WIFE of James D. Walkup
6. DATE OF BIRTH (month, day, and year) June 2-1905
7. AGE Years 32 Months 1 Days 20 If LESS than 1 day, hrs. or min.
OCCUPATION
8. Trade, profession, or particular kind of work done, as spinner, sawyer, bookkeeper, etc. housewife
9. Industry or business in which work was done, as silk mill, saw mill, bank, etc.
10. Date deceased last worked at this occupation (month and year)
11. Total time (years) spent in this occupation
12. BIRTHPLACE (city or town) (state or country) North Platte Nebraska
FATHER
13. NAME John H. Green
14. BIRTHPLACE (city or town) (State or country) Bloomington Illinois
MOTHER
15. MAIDEN NAME Storey Cannon Green
16. BIRTHPLACE (city or town) (State or country) Bloomington Illinois
17. INFORMANT James D. Walkup (Address)
18. BURIAL, CREMATION, OR REMOVAL Flagstaff Ariz. Date 7-26 1937
19. UNDERTAKER (Address) [illegible] Compton 1554
20. Filed 7-26 1937 [illegible] Registrar

MEDICAL CERTIFICATE OF DEATH
21. DATE OF DEATH (month, day, and year) 7/22/1937
22. I HEREBY CERTIFY, That I attended deceased from Found dead on road [illegible] alive on July 22 1937; death is said to have occurred on the date stated above, at 11 P. m.
The principal cause of death and related causes of importance were as follows: One gun shot wound in chest (front to back) in heart area by army rifle — Date of Onset 7-22-37.
Coroners jury investigated
Other contributory causes of importance: None
Name of operation Date of
What test confirmed diagnosis? Exam of body Was there an autopsy? No
23. If death was due to external causes (violence) fill in also the following:
Accident, suicide, or homicide? Suicide Date of injury 7-22-1937
Where did injury occur? 1 Mi. out Flagstaff Ariz.
(Specify city or town, county and State)
Specify whether injury occurred in industry, in home, or in public place. On side road
Manner of injury Gunshot wound
Nature of injury through chest (heart)
24. Was disease or injury in any way related to occupation of deceased? No
If so, specify
(Signed) [illegible] Miller Coroner
(Signed) [illegible] Ackerman M.D.
(Address) Flagstaff Ariz.
Back of Certificate to be used for any Additional Information

Marie Walkup's death certificate states she was found dead on a road from one shotgun wound to her chest. Note that no autopsy was done on her body nor on any of the children. *Courtesy of Karen Renner.*

the Walkups....She printed out the newspaper articles and took pictures of the gravesites and shared them with me....I was so glad she told me about it and that someone finally believed me.

Megan didn't just hear noises. She said she saw the kitchen drawers—one in particular—open and close on their own. At night as a child, when the noise became too disturbing, she would close her eyes and run downstairs to her parents' bedroom. She'd have to run past the kitchen, which could be terrifying. Megan said she'd then jump in bed between her mom and dad and pull up the covers. On some of those nights, a tiny figure would stand at the foot of her parents' bed for hours. She felt strongly that it was the spirit of a woman—although she's uncertain if it was Marie or Rose.

As an adult, Megan often stops by the house to see her father or take care of the plants and mail if he's out of town. She said she knows the spirits are still present— "I can feel the energy as soon as I open the door"—and has ambivalent feelings about letting her own children upstairs.

Of course, the house is much more than just a haunted place for me. I've had birthday parties there, celebrated holidays and had sleepovers when I was younger. I have a lot of happy memories of a normal life that happened

Left: An image of six-year-old Megan from the April 17, 1994 *Daily Sun* that was randomly shot by Sean Openshaw. Megan shared this photograph from the paper, which she has saved all these years. She feels a deep connection with the Walkup children from growing up in the house. *Courtesy of Megan Rawlinson Davis.*

Below: A taphophile (or cemetery tourist) would be intrigued by the Walkup family's grave marker. The plot itself is a double, with the children buried at one end and Marie at the other. *Author's collection.*

> *inside of it. But not a day goes by that I don't think of that house and how awful it was at night....It's made me stronger in my adult life, in coping with the different situations I've encountered.*

Later, I unpacked our conversation and thought about the house that had once been the scene of such tragedy. Megan's recounting of a childhood plagued by sleeplessness and terror took any romance out of the idea I had of living in a haunted house. Still, the desire to know who or what is opening those kitchen drawers and *why* persists, and I am intrigued. Could it be the spirit of Marie, searching for the icepick or looking for towels? Is she unable to break free from her past and so is doomed to exist in an energy loop that plays out repeatedly inside the house? The footsteps running up and down the narrow stairs—are they the echoes of the Walkup children in the days before the tragedy? So many questions and far too few answers.

I strongly suspect that Megan is a sensitive of sorts for whatever energy remains in the Leroux house. That none of the other family members were aware of the nightly chaos—or at least slept through it—tells me the connection is with her. She feels great empathy for the children and for Marie and told me she felt certain the children loved their mother very much. Megan shared a picture of herself as a child, taken by chance in 1994 by a photographer with the *Daily Sun*. She gave me permission to use it in this book, and I'm curious what the reader thinks of it.

Megan's account of growing up in the old house is by far the most vivid report of haunted activity there, but I came across a few others. A middle-aged man and his wife were speaking with me at an event, and he mentioned they had rented a house catty-corner from it when they were first married: "A couple of times I saw a young girl in a dress playing with a ball in the side yard. She'd chase it around to the front and then disappear. As far as I know, no little kids lived there then. I thought it was strange, but I figured it was the sunlight or I was tired."

Another woman's daughter was friends with Megan, and the mother told me the little girl "hated that house. She really thought it was haunted." As usual, neither of these people had been aware of the Walkup family and their tragic demise.

Ever since I first heard about the Walkup family of 1937, I've been fascinated by what's missing from the story. I still do research whenever I can on Marie and the children. However, since meeting Megan and hearing of her experiences, I've become even more interested in what or who is still living there.

CHAPTER 9

THEATRIKOS AND THE SITE OF THE BABBITT HOME

Everyone knows ghosts like to hang out in theaters, and Flagstaff's spirits are no exception. Winding up this exploration of the town's local haunts is a box-like structure that sits at the corner of North Beaver and Cherry. It's unusual for the area in that the building is two stories, with both a basement and an attic. Technically, Theatrikos is the name of the theater company and the Doris Harper-White Playhouse is the name of the place. However, say "Theatrikos" in town and people will point you toward the imposing building on the corner lot.

Long before community theater became part of Flagstaff's art scene, this piece of property belonged to Charles Babbitt, known around town as C.J. He was one of the five original Babbitt brothers who came out west in the early 1880s from Cincinnati, Ohio. The Babbitts were a well-educated, adventurous lot who left a life of wealth and ease to seek their fortunes as cattlemen. As the years passed, the brothers diversified and expanded their business holdings to automobiles, undertaking parlors, merchandising, banking—the list goes on. The Babbitts did quite well for themselves and for the town. Along with the Riordans, they were considered among the town fathers of the early twentieth century.[26]

Most of the brothers settled down in Flagstaff, raised families and tended to business. C.J. married a young woman from Cincinnati named Mary Verkamp and brought her out west. An interesting aside—in the same vein as the Riordans, three of the Babbitt brothers married three of the Verkamp sisters. Not only that, the Riordan wives Caroline and Elizabeth Metz were

The north face of Theatrikos. The far end of the building was used as a loading ramp, and it's said that in the 1970s, a desolate young man hanged himself from the rafters there. *Author's collection.*

cousins of the Babbitts from Ohio. This arrangement was not as unusual as it sounds today, and it did make for interesting politics in town.

According to historian Platt Cline, C.J. built a real Victorian castle on the West Cherry lot, complete with a three-story tower and a stone wall surrounding the property. A covered porch with white pillars curved around most of the front of the house, which was truly massive. Cline speculated that C.J. built the castle in 1900 in an attempt to appease his wife. Mary Verkamp was a lovely, vivacious young woman who had been quite a socialite in her native Cincinnati. C.J. was known as a quiet man, more at home on the range than in the public spotlight. There were those in town who found it hard to reconcile his image with the ostentatious mansion. Whatever the reason for building it, Mary Verkamp Babbitt ended up spending most of each year in Los Angeles with their children, returning to Flagstaff for the summers. After ten years, C.J. abandoned the castle and moved into a modest home in town. He continued living a quiet, unassuming life in Flagstaff until his death in 1956.

The property was turned into apartments in 1910. Years later it was used by the Elks Club, and later still, the building became a Union Hall. By 1964, the house had been through several renovations and was once again being used as apartments when a fire swept through and burned it to the ground. Nothing remains of the castle C.J. Babbitt built for his bride in 1900 except for the original stone wall battlement. Although crumbling in places, it still stands, defining the playhouse and its parking lot 120 years later.

The building erected on the lot after the fire swept through bears no resemblance to the castle. Until the early 1970s, it served again as a Laborers' Union Hall. It was about that time that the city began a search for a home for a new library. The old Babbitt property was chosen but only as a stopgap measure until funds were available for a dedicated building. Soon, the former Union Hall was filled with books, magazines, newspapers and the like. Librarians made the space work until 1987, when the current library was built on the site of the old Emerson School. It was then that Theatrikos took it over, changing the multilevel establishment into one of the better community theaters in Northern Arizona. While the current building has also been through renovations, it looks remarkably like it did in the 1980s.

The main entrance into the Doris Harper-White Playhouse is from the Cherry Street parking lot. Patrons climb the seven concrete steps and enter through one of two large doors into the lobby. Once upon a time, photographs and framed posters from past productions decorated the inside walls. The lobby itself is small for a theater and contains the requisite box office. It's also the space where patrons gather at intermission to mingle and sip refreshments. A doorway leads directly into a sizeable performance area, replete with permanent lighting, sound equipment, the stage and audience seating. Returning to the lobby, one could take a turn to the right and—instead of exiting the theater—descend a set of narrow, creepy stairs that lead into the building's basement. It's in this area that a former community player reported seeing the full-bodied apparition of a child running toward a door.

A flood in 2019 covered the basement in wastewater and destroyed many of the costumes, props and set pieces the company had accumulated over the years. Before that, the area was sectioned off and purposed into rooms with various names. The Green Room contained overstuffed chairs and a sofa, along with a monitor depicting the stage above. Actors could come down here between scenes to relax yet remain cued into the action of the performance. The Makeup Room was long, narrow and simple. Dominated

This photo was taken from the lobby door leading into the main theater. A volunteer was working near the stage one Saturday and looked up to see a partial apparition standing right about here. *Author's collection.*

by a back-lit mirror that ran its length, and a shelf that doubled as a vanity beneath, it served as a space of transformation for excited cast members. Nearby, a workshop with all the electric tools needed in building set pieces, scenery and so on was contained behind a locked enclosure. In the center of the basement, an open area was created and made available to community groups for acting lessons, improv games and rehearsals.

Finally, there was the Prop Room. Empty, it resembled little more than an elongated walk-in closet with shelving for an odd bit of clothing. However, long before the flood, those same shelves were jammed full of all kinds of delightful oddities and accessories. Obscure pieces of jewelry, lampshades, ash trays and candlesticks could be found behind a pile of wigs and scarves. Clothing from every period of the twentieth century was intermingled with any accessory imaginable to complete the required look. It was both magical and frustrating, depending on the search. While many items were throwaways—donated by families cleaning out a house—others were rare treasures. The flood that destroyed decades of collected oddities was devastating to Theatrikos.

After being thoroughly cleaned, the downstairs of the theater was reimagined and is now fully functional. The makeup room is almost twice as large, and a sliding door can divide it into two sections when needed. The Green Room is smaller but looks much the same. Both areas are a little brighter, with fresh coats of paint and furnishings. There is now a dedicated space used for rehearsals and the like and a small woodworking shop for constructing set design.

I spoke with a longtime Theatrikos member and volunteer, Jan Rominger, about her experiences at the theater:

> *I definitely feel there are spirits and ghosts that hang around the theater. While I haven't had any direct contact with one, I've been present when very strange things happen. For instance, we were putting on* A Christmas Carol *one year and were in rehearsal and having a terrible time with rigging the sound effects. I wanted the sound of Jacob Marley's chains rattling—but every time it cued up, the batteries would die. It happened repeatedly, and neither I nor our sound guy could figure it out. I was contemplating the situation when—*poof!*—the answer came right into my mind. Very strange! And the answer was—ask permission. So I did. I apologized to the spirit for being disruptive and explained I wanted the sound of rattling chains in the play, and could we please be allowed to proceed. We never had another problem with the batteries after that.*

Rominger also shared with me a photograph she thought was taken by a mother of a TheatriKid:

> *The mother was just snapping photographs of the set, the kids—nothing in particular. That night, after she was home, she was looking over the pictures when she came across one with the smoky white image of a lady sitting in the front row....I'm sure it's Theatrikos' "Victorian lady"—that's what I call her anyway.*

The spirit Rominger is referring to is the ghost of the old lady of the theater, and her presence is legendary. While this was the first—and likely only—image that's been captured, the lady has been seen in the audience before, dressed in stylish Victorian-era clothing and wearing a hat. She fades away when sighted by the actors and has never been seen during the actual play, just rehearsals. Her presence is benign and usually considered a sign of good luck.

A ghost of what's thought to be a child has been reported running across the theater's basement toward the exit. *Author's collection.*

I spoke to Sabine, the woman who snapped that iconic image, and she cleared up a few of the misconceptions that have taken root over the years:

> *It was in 2011, and the play was* Charlotte's Web. *I was actually there with the Cub Scouts....It wasn't a rehearsal; we brought the troop to watch*

> *the show. It hadn't started, and I wanted to take some pictures of the set, so I got up and walked toward the stage....I only snapped three pictures, and there were no people in any of the photos I took. I stood in front of where the audience sits....It wasn't until later, when I was home and looking at the pictures, that I saw the image of the old lady with her ornate hat watching the stage.*

I've seen the picture as well and was given permission to use it in this book. Sadly, because of the way it was formatted, it didn't meet the specifications necessary to reprint it. The photo is of a rural theater set with a colorful barn door and a large bale of hay positioned just outside it. The stage floor has been painted a grassy green. In the foreground of the image and below center stage, a blurry white image is plainly visible. While open to personal interpretation, the figure appears to me to be the head of a woman with a large hat perched atop her dark hair.

When I asked Sabine if she had felt anything eerie or paranormal when taking the picture, she replied, "I thought about it that night because the photo surprised me as much as anybody. But honestly, I didn't feel or think or notice anything out of the ordinary when I was up there taking the pictures. I just wanted to get them before the play started and go back to my seat."

Another spirit said to hang around the theater is not quite as pleasant as the old lady with the hat. This energetic presence seems to be that of a young male, and he's often felt as angry and disruptive. According to "Flagstaff's Haunted Places"—the self-guided tour written by James Hardy—this entity is often felt lurking near the north stairs to the basement. He's thought to be the spirit of a young man who, in the 1970s, hanged himself from the outside loading dock. An October 26, 2016 article in the *Daily Sun* reported a stage crew who experienced "a foreboding wave of fear" wash over them during a rehearsal. When the group decided it might be safer outside, they discovered that boxes of paper products had been tossed on the floor and a tipped refrigerator was blocking their exit. Other casts and crew have felt "an angry pair of eyes" watching from across the room or as they descend the stairway. Whether this one sad spirit is behind all the negative energy or is just an easy scapegoat is up for debate. However, it seems obvious that more than one entity has taken up residence in the theater.

Local ghost tours have reported orbs and unusual lights around Theatrikos's perimeter (not just the north stairs). Guides and tourists have taken photographs that show floating spheres of various sizes. Some of these orbs cluster above the remains of the original wall, often on the west side. They seem to be more active in summer.

One of the local performers said the theater had only recently installed a "ghost light" inside the building. He was referring to the black lights behind the stage, which are left on and cast an eerie shade of blue. For those who don't know, a ghost light is usually a single bulb that is left on whenever the theater is empty or otherwise dark. While there are many reasons for doing so, according to those who work onstage, a ghost light is there to appease the spirits of the theater. It may sound trite, but almost every playhouse from community theater to Broadway has its share of beloved ghosts who hang around. Some are content to watch rehearsals and interact with the living. Others interfere with the lights and sounds and in general make pests of themselves. Directors, performers and techs learn to work with them—as Rominger described earlier. While the black lights behind the main stage were not installed as a ghost light per se, they perform double duty at the theater.

Some locals have been active at Theatrikos for decades now and, like Rominger, have stories to tell. Mickey Mercer has acted, directed, volunteered and more, and he shared an incident that occurred in the mid-1990s:

> *I was directing a play,* The Glass Menagerie, *and there is a dramatic scene where a character throws his coat a few feet toward a chair. The coat is supposed to miss and accidentally hit a showcase where the miniature glass figurines are displayed, spilling them onto the floor. Then the two main characters pick up the pieces together and bond over the moment. Since it's pivotal to the play, we practiced it quite a bit—to get the coat throwing down right. On opening night, I was in the audience, and when it came to that scene, the actor threw his coat about five feet wide of the showcase. None of the miniature animal figures fell—which was disastrous for the action. The two actors were frozen in the moment before they began to recover….Probably ten seconds went by then, suddenly, the little figurines just fell over! Neither of the actors went near the showcase, there was no wind, no breeze….It was too long after the coat-throwing scene for any residual air to cause them to fall. I looked up and thanked the spirits of the theater. You know they're around even if you don't see them.*

Another seasoned actor, Paul Kulpinski, shared several of his encounters in the theater from the 1990s:

> *I've definitely had firsthand experiences with a spirit in Theatrikos, and I've also heard stories about others....The first project I did at the theater was in '92 for* A Christmas Carol. *I was rigging the lights, and I'd come in after hours to work, usually 10:00 p.m. to midnight. I was often alone, and after a few nights, I became aware of a presence....Later, I asked some of the cast members if Theatrikos had a ghost, and they all pretty much agreed that it did. To me, the spirit was of a young female, maybe eighteen to twenty-one years old. And she was just there to hang out and watch me work. I started to greet her every night I came in, telling her hello but asking her not to interrupt what I was doing...One Saturday, in 1992 or '93, I was working by myself on the main stage, and I noticed the light shift from the door to the lobby, like someone had come in from outside and needed my attention. I looked up and saw someone step into the doorway....I saw women's shoes and a dress that came to mid-calf that went up to the waist area—and then nothing! Once again, I had the sense this was a young woman...but she just vanished.*

Kulpinski had another experience when he was lighting the play *Sherlock's Last Case*. He said he felt the young woman's spirit was "heavily present" throughout the rehearsals leading up to the performances:

> *It was during the actual play, and this particular scene called for darkness. I was up in the booth, and I saw a dim blue light, about the size of a football, moving around on stage. I knew it wasn't coming from the houselights because I was manning them. I was panicky at first because I thought someone had a piece of iridescent tape stuck to their shirt or something...When the lighting changed, there was nothing there that could have caused the glowing blue orb. Two members of the cast told me they also saw it. Later, we heard that a strange thing happened in the theater kitchen that same night....The volunteers had individually wrapped cookies to sell at intermission, and the cookies began to fall off the counter, one by one, for no discernable reason.*

I was given an afternoon tour through the playhouse by John Propster and Suzanne Casale, two locals who are active there. It was mid-November, and the Christmas decorations were already up in the lobby while the set was being built for the seasonal play. As we poked around behind the main stage and downstairs, I recorded our conversations and took photos to examine later. For the most part, the building was deserted that day except for the three of us.[27]

Behind the curtain on center stage, the ghost light casts an eerie blue glow. Theatrikos member John Propster is not afraid of waking the spirits. *Author's collection.*

While sections of the theater are eerie—the cavernous main stage is dark, and footsteps echo ominously when it's empty—we encountered no ghostly figures on our tour. As said before, the basement has been renovated since the flood, with some spaces reconfigured and repurposed. Propster pointed out the changes but said that, even with the construction, he hasn't sensed anything paranormal. We walked through each room and talked about reported sightings from the past, but no entity showed its face. Later, when I had a chance to listen to the recording and check the images, I found nothing out of the ordinary. This is not surprising. My experience has shown me that ghostly encounters and paranormal events happen on their own time, not ours. Despite popular ghost-hunting programs depicting phenomena on demand, I believe the most credible sightings happen when people least expect them. However, going through buildings that have a haunted past can give a good baseline and appreciation of the space in which these events occurred.

CHAPTER 10
OTHER HAUNTS IN TOWN

Flagstaff is a city that has taken pains to preserve its historical roots, especially the downtown. As television shows like *Ghost Hunters* and *The Dead Files* have become increasingly popular, the city has seen an influx of visitors who want to explore its hidden secrets and hopefully connect with a ghost or two. It's only natural to presume that one-hundred-year-old buildings remain attractive to the spirits of those who lived their lives within them. There are many more structures throughout town that have hauntings attached to them than the nine detailed in this book. Below are a few more that the inquisitive paranormal investigator can delve into on her own.

CRYSTAL MAGIC

This lovely New Age gift shop sells not only crystals but also candles, tarot cards, teapots, jewelry and more. It sits at the corner of San Francisco and Route 66 and has been in business for thirty years. Locals who have worked inside swear there is a dark entity that inhabits the basement and tries to frighten employees who are sent down there to restock. A downstairs bathroom is also said to attract an unhappy spirit, and employees avoid the area as much as possible.

The structure has a storied history. Known today as the James Vail Building, it was the popular Parlor Saloon at the turn of the twentieth century. A wealthy entrepreneur, Vail died by suicide in 1906 after a wagon accident left him with a crushed leg.

In the early 1900s, the downtown businesses were connected by a series of underground passageways known as "the Tunnels." Today, they have achieved mythological status and pique the interest of ghost hunters and historians alike. While they were first built to carry steam and heat the buildings, evidence has been found to link them to illegal gambling and opium use. The basement at Crystal Magic was part of the labyrinth, but all the tunnels were blocked off well before 2021. However, many psychics have held that darker spirits reside in the Tunnels and do not like being disturbed.

THE MILLIGAN HOUSE

The old Milligan house is now used as offices by the Flagstaff Convention and Visitors Bureau. A mural of Mabel Milligan climbing the stairs is on a wall inside the red brick home. *Author's collection.*

This beautiful brick building presently houses the Flagstaff Convention and Visitors Bureau offices. It's located across the street from the public library and is the former home of J.C. Milligan. Milligan was the owner of a brickyard as well as justice of the peace in the late 1890s. He was once described as a blustery German who routinely stood outside on his front lawn, yelling at the children across the street at Emerson School.

However, the hauntings reported within the home aren't from J.C. but rather his daughter Mabel, who died in her upstairs bedroom. Mabel Milligan was a woman ahead of her time, a teacher who took travel assignments to the Four Corners area. She never married, and between teaching stints, she would return to her parents' home. Mabel had diabetes, and one evening in 1923, she slipped into a coma and died in her sleep.

Mabel is a friendly ghost who makes her presence known by flipping lights on and off, walking up the stairs and interfering with staff's computers. She is also said to be possessive of the kitchen and dislikes electric coffee makers;

none work properly in there and must be moved to a neutral area. Mural Mice painted a lifelike image of Mabel on a south wall, which depicts her ascending the staircase with a candle.[28]

Mother Road Brewing Company

South of the tracks on Mikes Pike is Mother Road, a locally owned, independent brewery. While known for its craft beers, community spirit and outside venue, those who have worked there also know it as haunted.

Mother Road is aptly named after old Route 66, which ran right alongside the brewery's present location. However, the paranormal activity doesn't arise from America's historic road. According to former employees, there are shadow spirits that reside among the outside seating. The reports are of visual entities that dart about at night, sometimes accompanied by chills or feelings of dread by the living. Although I haven't been able to verify this, it's said the land Mother Road sits on was once the site of the town's only laundromat. This would have been at the turn of the century (1900s), and the facility was responsible for cleaning sheets from the hospitals as well as anything from the lumber mill. Body parts from unfortunate accident victims were often rolled up in the linen and, when received by the launderers, were buried among the trees.

Riordan Mansion

Also south of the tracks and abutting NAU is Riordan Mansion State Park. This land contains the former home of Timothy and Michael Riordan, who, along with the Babbitts, were considered the town fathers. The brothers owned and ran the lumber mills and played a hand in forming almost every political and cultural entity of their day. The thirteen-thousand-square-foot Arts and Crafts–style mansion was built in 1904 and consists of two homes that are connected by a common room, often called the ballroom. The two Riordan brothers married two sisters, Caroline and Elizabeth Metz, and during the lumber mill's heyday, the large home was a busy place. Both men kept extensive diaries, as did some of their offspring. While there were plenty of parties and dances at the mansion, there was great sadness too.

Riordan Mansion State Historic Park gives tours through the 1904 Arts and Crafts–style homes of Tim and Michael Riordan. Visitors can freely roam the grounds around the building and visit the remains of the faerie circle. *Author's collection.*

The polio epidemic hit Flagstaff in the 1920s, as it did towns all over the United States. In September 1927, Michael Riordan's son Arthur felt poorly and left his job at the bank, walking several blocks home. Later that evening, his cousin Anna, daughter of Tim and Caroline, fell suddenly ill, and both young adults deteriorated rapidly. They died before morning, and because of polio's infectious nature, their bodies were left at the house until quarantine was lifted. The Riordans were grief-stricken but found the strength to carry on. Today, there are rumors that the spirit of Anna never left.

While some guides at the park are dismissive, others have admitted to reports of paranormal phenomena in the east home, which belonged to Tim and Caroline. A woman was touring the mansion in the 2000s, and the group was on the second floor. Upon entering Anna's bedroom, she distinctly felt the presence of a young female who was watching the tour with some amusement. Objects have been moved from the bookshelves, and the light kept on in the second-floor chapel has flickered and danced without a breeze evident. That same light was said to have burned out abruptly on the day of Caroline's death in 1943.[29]

The Riordans were an Irish Catholic family from Chicago who were very active in the church. However, even Tim Riordan indulged in a bit of mythical whimsy when building their home. He constructed a faerie circle a few yards away from the house, the remains of which are still there today.

NORTHERN ARIZONA UNIVERSITY

I've noticed that almost every university across the United States has a ghost story attached to it, and NAU is no exception. Morton Hall and McConnell Hall receive the most attention, and several hauntings are attributed to each.

Morton Hall is located on north campus and is part of the original university. It was built in 1918, as were many of the old brick buildings that make up this part of NAU. It's been a home for students over the decades and has seen its share of heartbreak. The most widely circulated ghost sighting connected to Morton regards Kathy, a young student from the 1950s who was forced to stay in Flagstaff over Christmas vacation. As sad as that made her, something far worse occurred during the holiday, at least to her twenty-year-old mind: Kathy's boyfriend ended their relationship. Bereft and alone, Kathy hanged herself from a second-floor window. In the decades that followed, her ghost has been seen floating down hallways

Morton Hall still stands on NAU's northern campus. Past residents insist it's haunted by the spirit of Kathy. *Author's collection.*

and lingering by the window she used in her death. There have also been reports of radio interference in the dorm, with stations spontaneously changing to '50s swing music. In the years since Kathy's death, students have complained of knocking on walls, the sudden scent of roses and toilets that flush themselves. Whether true or not, these eerie occurrences are usually attributed to her restless spirit.

McConnell Hall, located in south campus, is comparatively modern and was built in the 1970s. It is located very close to Calvary Cemetery, and there are (unfounded) rumors the university appropriated a few acres of burial land from the Catholic diocese to expand the campus. That said, past residents of the hall say they frequently experienced phenomena such as scratching sounds, whispers, footsteps in empty hallways and singing. Most unsettling are the apparitions of a man and several children who wander through the dorm, oblivious to the students who live there. These sightings have been reported throughout the past three decades with no clues to the spirits' origins.[30]

THE MUSEUM CLUB

Probably the most haunted building in the minds of Flagstaffians is the Museum Club. This country western bar has been part of the town for almost a century and is located several miles east, off old Route 66. The building's rich history began with taxidermist Dean Eldredge, who needed a place to showcase his animals. In 1931, he built what he called "the biggest log cabin in the world" and operated the place as a museum. Its reputation grew as it expanded into a trading post, and the "Zoo" became a favorite stop of tourists traveling the Mother Road. Doc Williams bought the building after Eldredge died in '36 and reopened it as a nightclub. The Zoo survived through the years as a musical venue, but when Don Scott bought it in the 1960s, he turned it into a country western bar, and the scene exploded. Waylon Jennings, Willie Nelson, Barbara Mandrell—one never knew who would show up at the Zoo.

Don Scott and his wife, Thorna, lived in an apartment above the bar, but in 1973, tragedy struck. One night after closing the venue, Thorna was climbing the steps to their home when she tripped and fell down the

The Museum Club is famous throughout the West (some would say the world). Ask a local about haunted buildings, and the Zoo is usually the first place mentioned. *Author's collection.*

stairs. She died a few weeks after, never regaining consciousness. Don was inconsolable, and several years later, he shot himself near the fireplace.[31]

The Museum Club continued to thrive under the management of the Zanzucchi family, but employees and patrons suspect the Scotts are still hanging around their beloved Zoo. Apparitions of a woman have been seen at day and night wandering through the downstairs bar. Many believe it's Thorna, and she's been known to slip into a booth beside a stranger before disappearing in a haze. Thorna also plays havoc with bottles and glasses behind the bar—switching the whiskeys, knocking over drinks and opening cupboard doors. Locals driving past the club in the early morning hours have reported seeing flickering lights inside the building. Footsteps have been heard going up and down the stairs when no one's about, and employees have felt like they were being watched when closing the bar.

The Museum Club is a great place for the aspiring ghost hunter to start in Flagstaff. A search online will also give sites where locals have posted videos and pictures of unexplained phenomena from inside the bar.

THE MCMILLIAN BUILDING

Erected in 1888 by Thomas McMillian, this building located across Old 66 from the train depot was a two-story bank and hotel. McMillian is generally acknowledged as Flagstaff's first white settler. Originally from Tennessee, he came through Flagstaff on Beale's Road, driving his sheep toward California. The clean mountain air and lush green pastures made an impression in his mind, and when a drought hit California, he drove his flock back this way. Besides buildings and roads, McMillian Mesa bears the name of Flagstaff's original pioneer.

In 2022, the McMillian Building contains a popular restaurant/bar downstairs, while the upstairs is divided into offices. It's on the second floor that shadow figures, doors opening and closing on their own and footsteps echoing down empty halls have been reported. Casual ghost hunting was not encouraged when I poked around the top floor in 2019. However, one tenant did speak to me about the "occasional" phenomena he had encountered since renting an office there:

> *I don't really believe in haunted houses or buildings, but I'll admit that I've heard footsteps coming down the hall when I'm absolutely sure I'm alone*

> *up here. It freaked me out the first time and, fortunately, doesn't happen often. It's an old building, so maybe there's a rational explanation for the sounds.... That's what I tell myself anyway.*

There are other businesses and houses in town that have stories attached. Much like the McMillian Building, Flagstaff is an old town. It's full of history, and many of its structures are well preserved. It's easy to believe that those who came before might want to come back now and then to check in on the place they helped create.

You have probably noticed in reading this book that some of the same types of ghosts make an appearance at different locations in town. That's not to discredit any of the hauntings or sightings. It makes sense that ghosts in the shape of men or women would have vague features and be difficult to distinguish from one another. When it comes to telling their stories (as on a ghost tour), location and action are important identifiers. Whose ghost could this be, dancing in the hotel ballroom? Which spirits might be attached to the train station or find solace walking the rails? For me as well as for many others, it's the stories from the past that tie the sightings from today together.

The afterword, by Dr. Karen Renner, explores some common paranormal phenomena and the stories behind them. It's interesting that descriptions of these ghostly apparitions are often the same in towns separated by thousands of miles. Whether this is our shared mythology or more evidence of life after death I leave up to the reader. I hope you've found the stories enjoyable and learned some of the history behind Arizona's mountain town, Flagstaff.

AFTERWORD

DEBUNKING THE MYTHS

BY DR. KAREN RENNER

I first met Susan during the summer of 2019. I had been working at Northern Arizona University since 2010, teaching and writing about American literature and popular culture. That summer, I was invited to serve as the writer in residence for the Flagstaff Public Library. Part of that work included giving a presentation for the library's "Local Legends" series. As a horror scholar, it only made sense that I would look at our town's ghost stories. This research very quickly led me to Susan, as it was obvious from her business, Freaky Foot Tours, that she was a local expert. Susan and I then collaborated on the presentation.[32]

I would call myself a hopeful skeptic. I spend a lot of time watching YouTube footage claiming to provide evidence of the paranormal, whether in the form of aliens, cryptids or ghosts. Most of these videos are too dark or blurry to offer much in the way of proof. Others are more convincing, but in this day of Photoshop, it's easy to dismiss those as clever fakes.

Most of the time, though, I'm paying more attention to the way the stories are framed: who the ghosts are, where they appear and to whom and why they are said to still be lingering in our world. Embedded in these stories, I see a variety of hopeful beliefs—that victims are not forgotten, that our souls outlive our bodies and that science will never explain away all the wonder and mysteries of our world.

When I first heard about the various ghosts that haunted Flagstaff, I began looking for historical evidence of their origin stories. I wanted to name the prostitutes pushed out the windows of the Monte Vista. I wanted to know who the elderly woman was who rocks the chair in room 305 and why she had been a long-term guest of the hotel. I wanted to understand why a man killed his new bride and then himself in the Weatherford. I believed that if I knew more about who these people were, I'd be able to understand why they had made such an impression on the living.

I never found out their names. In fact, I never found any evidence that these events had actually taken place. What I did find was far more interesting.

Flagstaff isn't the only place where the ghosts of prostitutes harass guests, especially men. The spirits of these "ladies in red" are actually rather common. So, for that matter, are the apparitions of wronged brides, often referred to as "women in white," and the spirits of old ladies in rocking chairs. In most cases, the historical facts about the identities of these female ghosts are as fuzzy as the supposed YouTube evidence of them.

LADIES IN RED

The so-called oldest profession is unfortunately also one of the most dangerous, so tales of murdered prostitutes and their angry ghosts are sadly a rather common occurrence, especially in towns that once housed a booming bordello or two—as many of the towns in the West did.

Only one source that I could find gave any specific details about the murdered prostitutes of the Monte Vista. In *Red Light Women of the Rocky Mountains*, Jan MacKell writes that two prostitutes "were supposedly murdered on the third floor of the hotel during the 1940s and their bodies thrown out of the window." MacKell does not cite a source for this story, and her use of the word *supposedly* suggests we are in the realm of rumor and speculation.

A similar story set in the Adolphus Hotel in Dallas, Texas, has a bit more substance, though. In a 2018 article, S. Holland Murphy reports that in 1959, "the 'smashed body' of a 25-year-old prostitute was found in a small courtyard 14 floors below her room. The *News* described the woman's body plunging down the '4×8 inset in the building, ricocheting from wall to wall.'" A *New York Times* article from 1977 by Selwyn Raab describes a prostitute who was "killed in a mysterious plunge last July from the 10th floor of a shabby midtown hotel." The most shocking part of the story is that the girl was only twelve.

However, a lack of historical grounding doesn't prevent comparable tales from popping up. The website for Old Town Brewing and Pizza in Portland,

Oregon, actually has a name for its ghostly lady of the evening: Nina. It even explains how to properly pronounce her name (with a long *i*). According to the website, Nina shared information about the white slavery market, which was apparently thriving in the city at the time (though when that was exactly is unclear). In retaliation, Nina was murdered—thrown not out of a window but down an elevator shaft. She supposedly still haunts the premises, signaling her presence with "a faint waft of perfume." The Rawls Hotel in Alabama has a lady in red as well. In 2016, Josh Boutwell, writing for the *Dothan Eagle*, claimed that the apparition often appears near the second-story stairs "where she was reportedly shoved from the balcony to her death."

Similar narratives can be found in fiction, too. The origin story of Catwoman in Tim Burton's 1992 film *Batman Returns*, for example, features Selina Kyle, played by Michelle Pfeiffer, being pushed out of a window. Though Pfeiffer's Kyle is a mousy secretary rather than a streetwalker, Catwoman has long been associated with sex work, with her iconic outfit recalling the garb of a dominatrix. More recently, the HBO series *The Deuce* (2017–19) also featured the tragic defenestration of a prostitute.

Lest we forget, the lady in red has a biblical precedent, too, in the figure of Jezebel, whose name has come to be a euphemism for a prostitute. Jezebel suffered a far worse fate than most ladies in red, though: after being pushed out of a window, she was then trampled by horses and eaten by dogs. Yikes.

LADIES IN WHITE

The lady in red has a purer counterpart, the so-called lady in white. In *Haunted Colleges and Universities of Massachusetts*, Renee Mallett writes that "lady in white hauntings are something of a universal ghostly archetype. As the name implies, this kind of ghost is seen as a white-clad woman; some stories go so far as to describe her as wearing a wedding dress. Her story is usually one of lost love or betrayal by her fiancé or newlywed husband."

Flagstaff's version haunts the Weatherford Hotel, the ghost of a bride who, depending on the source, was either killed by her husband on her honeymoon or hanged herself when her husband left and did not return. In some versions, the husband was killed, while in others, he simply abandoned her.

Although I have found no historical grounding for the Weatherford's story, two hotels on different sides of the country date the tragic deaths of their women in white to 1927, so some actual event may have inspired at least some of these ghostly tales. Multiple sources point to a tragedy that took place in 1927 at the Red Coach Inn in Niagara Falls. Supposedly, a newlywed couple checked into the hotel, and the next morning, the bride was found bludgeoned to death in her bed.

Meanwhile, as Parker Anderson and Darlene Wilson explain in *Haunted Prescott*, another book in this series, that town's Hassayampa Inn has a legend about "a newlywed bride named Faith Summers and her groom [who] checked into room 426 on their wedding night, very shortly after the hotel opened in 1927." Supposedly, Faith's husband went out for cigarettes and never returned, and after a few days, Faith hanged herself.

Although the Adolphus was the site of the tragic murder of a prostitute, as discussed earlier, it's a woman in white who is said to haunt its premises—yet another jilted bride, and from around the same time. According to its website, the woman "was due to be married one day during the 1930s, but her fiancé didn't show, leaving the bride-to-be embarrassed and broken-hearted. Later that day her body was found, hanging a few feet from the spot where she was due to say her vows."

The woman in white who haunts the Omni Homestead Resort in Virginia, on the other hand, fits the jilted bride version of the tale. According to the website Historic Hotels of New York, "Her groom-to-be had become plagued by second thoughts. On the day of their wedding, the groom instructed the young woman to wait in her hotel room while he ran out for a quick errand. Unfortunately, for the bride, her beloved was never to return. Distraught, she took her own life." Room 19 in the historic Jefferson Hotel in Texas houses a similar spirit, "a bride that hanged herself from this very bed because her husband did not show to the wedding," according to its website. The website for the Hotel Alex Johnson in South Dakota dates the passing of its woman in white to the 1970s, when supposedly a young bride jumped out the window of room 812. However, according to the website, many suspected foul play.

Whether driven to suicide by the shame of rejection or murdered outright by their husbands, women in white traipse the hallways of lots of hotels across America. Other stories can be found at the Paranormal Database website, which dedicates an entire page to "Phantom Brides and Related Myths."

MATRIARCHAL GHOSTS

The ghosts of elderly women in rocking chairs also abound. These women are often said to be owners or—like the woman who haunts room 305 in Flagstaff's Hotel Monte Vista—at least long-term residents. So common are such figures that Mark Leslie devoted a whole chapter to "The Rocking Chair Ghost" in *Tomes of Terror: Haunted Bookstores and Libraries*. Also, anyone who has ridden on Disneyland's Haunted Mansion ride might remember the ghost of an old woman rocking back and forth near a fireplace in the Grand Hall.

The Baldpate Inn in Estes Park, Colorado, is said to be haunted by Ethel Mace, a former owner. According to VisitEstesPark.com, "Ethel can be seen sitting in her rocker on the porch, admiring the views." Similarly, the Gregory House in Bodie, California, is also said to house the ghost of an old woman, whom guests and staff have reported seeing sitting in a rocking chair, knitting an afghan. In a 2016 article in *Mountain Living*, Heidi Kerr-Schlaefer wrote that one of the namesakes of the Hand Hotel Bed and Breakfast in Fairplay, Colorado, still calls the place home: "Grandma Hand is said to haunt the room that bears her name, and when her chair is rocking back and forth all by itself, you know she's home."

This type of ghost isn't limited to the West, though. In *Haunted Lawrence*, Paul Thomas describes the ghost of an older woman who haunts an unspecified house on Rhode Island Street. Thomas writes that she "sits in a rocking chair and peers out of the building's south window. According to the homeowners, 'She sits in her rocker as though watching the world pass by,'" a description that sounds eerily similar to what is said of the old woman in the Monte Vista. Alan Brown, in *The Haunted South*, says that a similar ghost is said to inhabit the Magnolia Manor Bed and Breakfast in South Carolina.

That such similar stories have cropped up in a large number of locations across the country suggests to me that these stories might be better classified as urban legends. But as a hopeful skeptic, I wait to be happily proven wrong.

—Dr. Karen J. Renner
Associate Professor, English
Northern Arizona University

Notes

Introduction

1. Flagstaff's early Anglo history is well documented in several books, most notably those written by Platt Cline. In the introduction as well as chapter 1, information has been gathered from multiple sources that are interconnected and intertwined to the extent that it's impossible to credit any one of them.

Chapter 1

2. Arizonans were known as a cantankerous lot. Kgun9.com out of Tucson had a good posting titled "The Long Road to Arizona's Statehood," published February 14, 2021.
3. Cline, *Mountain Town*, chs. 1 and 2.
4. The *Coconino Sun* was the town's weekly newspaper until 1946, when it changed its name to the *Arizona Daily Sun* and became a daily paper. Anything and everything that went on in this small mountain town was published somewhere inside. The paper has been a great source for researching and gaining insight into Flagstaff's early years. As of 2021, issues of the *Coconino Sun* until 1927 can be found online at the Library of Congress site.

Chapter 2

5. Cline, *Mountain Town*, chs. 2 and 3.
6. I first read the story about the murderous janitor in a pamphlet compiled by James Hardy for the Flagstaff Visitors Bureau. It was one of the city's self-guided

walking tours, this one being on the town's haunted buildings. Since reading it, some ten years ago, I've heard the same story retold by locals, always with their own embellishments.

7. I'm no expert on orbs or EVPs, but I've been told by others who profess to be that the whole area where the library is—including the Rio de Flag and Wheeler Park—has a lot of paranormal activity. I've seen pictures and video of some of the orbs, and they are impressive.
8. I first heard of the hanging tree some fifteen years ago on a local tour, but I've never found definite proof it was in what is now the library parking lot. However, historian James Hardy told a *Daily Sun* reporter in an October 13, 2007 interview that when he went to Emerson School, the story was that the janitor buried his family beneath said tree after he murdered them.

Chapter 3

9. Information on John Weatherford and his Majestic Opera House and Weatherford Hotel can be found in Cline's book *Mountain Town*, 152–53, as well as *Historic Tales of Flagstaff* by Schindler and Kitt and the Weatherford Hotel's website.
10. I was honored to have participated in a short segment of the *Dead File* program exploring haunted Flagstaff. While unable to disclose particular sightings and/or discoveries, I will say I heard more stories from locals about ghosts and paranormal encounters than I'd known existed. The whole experience solidified my thoughts on Flagstaff as being a place where old spirits still roam the downtown.

Chapter 4

11. Schindler and Kitt wrote a whole chapter on Weatherford's "folly" in their book *Historic Tales of Flagstaff*.
12. Wikipedia, "Zane Grey."
13. Zane Grey's comings and goings in town were well documented by the *Coconino Sun*. One gets the idea that Mr. Grey made his opinions known and enjoyed talking to anyone and everyone, including the reporters of the day.
14. As I mentioned in the acknowledgements, when it comes to relaying stories of paranormal sightings or occurrences, I only use a person's full name if they've agreed to such. Some people have not; others I haven't been able to find or get in touch with. However, I have extensive notes going back almost a decade on some stories I've been told or heard secondhand.
15. Easton had hoped to publish her paper, but for now it remains with her. She also explores several hauntings at NAU in it.
16. The self-guided walking tour from the visitors' center details several of the hauntings reported at the Weatherford, as well as a few lesser-known incidents.

Chapter 5

17. Platt Cline was a friend of the good doctor, and it was in his book *Mountain Town*, 413–15, that I found the most detailed descriptions of Dr. Raymond.

Chapter 6

18. Leo Bart's grave site, along with his tragically brief bio, was part of an October 8, 2017 fundraiser for Northern Arizona Pioneers' Historical Society. The group puts together self-guided headstone history tours periodically, and it always make for an interesting afternoon.
19. Besides the 2009 *Sun* article, Hardy's self-guided tour mentions the locked/unlocked door phenomenon, as well as staff seeing and hearing unexplained noises, shadows and so on in the depot.
20. According to a 2018 article from jackcentral.org, there have been over seventy fatalities from trespassers on the rails as of June 30, 2018. Flagstaff police attribute some of those to suicide; however, accidental deaths involving alcohol intoxication rank high in those numbers. Also, those seventy-plus deaths are only from "trespassers" and don't include accidents involving railroad workers.

Chapter 7

21. The Hotel Monte Vista has an extensive website with its history, reported hauntings, great pictures and much more that's available online. Historical background on the hotel has been taken from there, as well as Cline's book *Mountain Town* and early issues of the *Coconino Sun.*
22. Flagstaff's near chance of becoming the haven of big movie studios and filmdom is also detailed on the website discoverHollywood.com.
23. One of Flagstaff's more respected madams was Dutch May Peters, who owned at least two brothels on south San Francisco in the early 1900s. She and her partner/husband (it's unclear which) came to a grisly end on September 1, 1916. The town was outraged by the couple's murder, as Dutch May was well liked, paid her taxes and didn't stand for "rabble-rousing."

Chapter 8

24. In 2021, *Flagstaff's Walkup Family Murders: A Shocking 1937 Tragedy* was written by this author and published by The History Press. I gathered information on the family mainly from past issues of the *Coconino Sun*. A graduate student at NAU, Keith Robinson, also wrote a paper on the tragedy that rocked this small town decades ago. That paper, "No Milk Today," now resides in NAU's Special Collections at Cline Library.
25. Megan Rawlinson Davis contacted me after the *Daily Sun* wrote an article on the Walkup book publication. We talked for hours one night, and the stories she told

me of growing up inside that house during the 1980s and '90s were as disturbing as they were fascinating. I had no idea of the extent of hauntings inside when I wrote my first book on the family.

Chapter 9

26. The Babbitt brothers and their families played such a huge role in Flagstaff's early stability and growth that it's difficult to find an area they didn't contribute to. They were merchants, of course, but also civic-minded and family oriented and, along with the Riordans in the 1900s, as close to being the town fathers as Flagstaff had. Platt Cline's *Mountain Town* details much of the family's history, and the Babbitts have published several accounts themselves. Richard and Sherry Mangum's *Flagstaff: Past and Present* also contributed to my knowledge on the family and C.J.'s house.
27. This chapter was by far the easiest to write, as so many volunteers and performers from Theatrikos came forward with their stories. Many thanks to all those who responded and allowed me to share their experiences in this book.

Chapter 10

28. Hardy's walking tour pamphlet has a paragraph or so on Mabel. However, I felt like I got to know her through the pages of the *Coconino Sun*. I also spoke to several staff members of the CVB who repeated Hardy's stories.
29. It would be hard to over-stress the importance of the Riordan family in the history of Flagstaff. Like the Babbitts, their lives were intertwined with the growth of the town, and it would take some space to list all their contributions. The family's history is available in Cline's book, as well as on the Riordan Mansion State Historic Park website.
30. While the legends that haunt NAU are best known and propagated by the local grapevine, two short articles on the campus's ghosts were found on flagstaffurbanlegends.wordpress.com.
31. Both the history of the Museum Club and the hauntings reported within have been documented extensively throughout the decades. The reader can trace the building's many transformations in back issues of the *Daily Sun*, and the bar's website keeps tabs on the paranormal phenomena captured and reported.

Afterword

32. As Karen Renner did an excellent job of noting her sources in the text, I have only added her sources to the bibliography.

BIBLIOGRAPHY

Newspapers

Arizona Daily Sun
Coconino Sun
Dothan Eagle
New York Times

Books and Articles

Anderson, Parker, and Darlene Wilson. *Haunted Prescott*. Charleston, SC: The History Press, 2018.

Babbitt, James E., and John G. DeGraff III. *Flagstaff*. Charleston, SC: Arcadia Publishing, 2009.

Brown, Alan. *The Haunted South*. Charleston, SC: Arcadia Publishing, 2014.

Cline, Platt. *Mountain Town, Flagstaff's First Century*. Flagstaff, AZ: Northland Publishing, 1994.

Easton, Madison. "Newly Formed Team of Female Ghost Hunters Begin Their Journey into the Investigating and Healing of a Haunted Flagstaff." 2022.

Hardy, James. "Flagstaff's Haunted Places: Self-Guided Historic Walking Tour." Written for Discover Flagstaff/Flagstaff Visitors Center, circa 2009.

Johnson, Susan. *Flagstaff's Walkup Family Murders: A Shocking 1937 Tragedy*. Charleston, SC: The History Press, 2021.

Leslie, Mark. *Tomes of Terror: Haunted Bookstores and Libraries*. Tkaronto, CAN: Dundurn Press, 2014.

MacKell, Jan. *Red Light Women of the Rocky Mountains*. Albuquerque: University of New Mexico Press, 2009.

Magnum, Richard, and Sherry Magnum. *Flagstaff Past & Present*. Flagstaff, AZ: Northland Publishing, 2003.

Mallett, Renee. *Haunted Colleges and Universities of Massachusetts*. Charleston, SC: The History Press, 2013.
Northern Arizona Pioneers' Historical Society. "Calvary Catholic Cemetery Tour: Who Lies Beneath?" October 8, 2017.
Riordan Mansion, State Historic Park. "Self-Guided Walk."
Schindler, Kevin, and Michael Kitt. *Historic Tales of Flagstaff.* Charleston, SC: The History Press, 2019.
Thomas, Paul. *Haunted Lawrence.* Charleston, SC: The History Press, 2017.

Websites

Church, Kelly. "NAU's McConnell Hall." December 11, 2011. flagstaffurbanlegends.wordpress.com.
Discover Flagstaff. www.flagstaffarizona.org.
Estes Park Colorado. visitestespark.com.
Grosvenor, Jake, and Mary Ann Witt. "NAU Students Mourn the Loss of Their Friend." August 31, 2018. jackcentral.org.
Historic Hotels of New York. historichotels.org.
Historic Jefferson Hotel. historicjefferson.com.
Hoglund, Krista. "NAU's Morton Hall." December 11, 2011. flagstaffurbanlegends.wordpress.com.
Hotel Alex Johnson. alexjohnson.com.
Hotel Monte Vista. hotelmontevista.com.
Kerr-Schlaefer. mountainliving.com.
Kgun9.com (Tucson).
Old Town Pizza and Brewing. Otbrewing.com.
The Paranormal Database. Paranormaldatabase.com.
Weatherford Hotel. weatherfordhotel.com.
Weatherford Hotel. YouTube, youtu.be/5x1iHUR2pgM.
Wikipedia. "Zane Grey." en.m.wikipedia.org.

About the Author

Susan Johnson has lived in her adopted hometown of Flagstaff for over thirty years. She loves searching out forgotten tales and hidden stories on the people who brought this town to life centuries ago. With her son, Nick, as manager, Susan helps with Freaky Foot Tours, looking for new haunts to share with others.

Besides writing and scaring tourists with ghost stories, she enjoys hiking the trails with her corgi, Shimmer.